FOUR MONTHS AFOOT IN SPAIN

With bag and baggage

FOUR MONTHS
AFOOT IN SPAIN

BY

HARRY A. FRANCK

AUTHOR OF "A VAGABOND JOURNEY AROUND THE WORLD."

ILLUSTRATED
WITH PHOTOGRAPHS

NEW YORK
THE CENTURY CO.

A FOREWORD

YET another story of travels in western Europe, especially one having for its basis the mere random wanderings of a four-months' absence from home, may seem almost to call for apology. If so, it is hereby duly tendered. What befell me on this vacation jaunt is no story of harrowing adventure, nor yet a record of the acquisition of new facts. But as I covered a thousand miles of the Iberian peninsula on foot, twice that distance by third-class rail, and am given to mingling with "the masses," it may be that there have filtered into the following pages some facts and impressions that will be new to the reader. Yet it is less to record these that I have written, than to answer a question that has often been put to me since my return:

"How can a man make such a journey on $172?"

THE AUTHOR.

CONTENTS

CHAPTER   PAGE

   I. A 'Tweendecks Journey 3

  II. Footpaths of Andalusia 28

 III. The Last Foothold of the Moor . . 52

 IV. The Banks of the Guadalquivir . . . 72

  V. The Torero at Home 89

 VI. Tramping Northward 115

 VII. Spanish Roads and Roadsters 132

VIII. On the Road in La Mancha 145

 IX. The Trail of the Priest 157

  X. Shadows of the Philips 171

 XI. Crumbling Cities 198

 XII. Wildest Spain 217

XIII. The Land of the Basque 243

XIV. A Descent Into Aragon 264

 XV. Emigrating Homeward 275

LIST OF ILLUSTRATIONS

	PAGE
With bag and baggage	*Frontispiece*
Showing The Author's Itinerary	4
A street in terraced Gibraltar	13
"The Road to Spain"	33
A company of "guardias civiles"	48
A cork factory	48
A Moorish gate of Ronda	55
A fishman of Malaga	58
A Spanish highway	58
The so-called "King of the Gipsies"—Granada . .	67
A Spanish railway station	70
A gitana of Granada	75
In the district of the Alhambra	75
Ubiquitous features of Spanish church architecture .	78
A Sevillian street	97
The Plaza, San Fernando	102
" A'ua! A'ua fresca! Quien quiere beber? " .	102
Above all Seville bulks the cathedral and la Giralda .	107
Photographed by D. Anderson, Rome.	
The Golden Tower on the Guadalquivir . . .	107
A bull-fight as it is not. Goya's impressionistic caricature	112
Photographed by D. Anderson, Rome.	
Cordoba's deceptive entrance	117
Suburban life in Spain	117
A herd of fighting bulls	124
The peasants' noonday	124
Farming in old Castile	131
In the market district	142

LIST OF ILLUSTRATIONS

PAGE

One of Spain's great rivers — nearly knee-deep . . 149

A street 156

A wind-swept village 161

A bridge over the Tajo — Toledo . . . 161

"Toledo la rica" 164

The sun-dodging streets of Toledo . . . 166

La Puerta del Sol, Madrid: the Spaniard's center of the
universe 171

The Manzanares, Madrid's only river . . . 173

"Los borrachos"—Velasquez 176

An Alameda by day, chairs stacked until busy night-time. 181

Faustino Posadas 188

A Spanish city's water-supply 188

Much bridge and little river — Madrid . . . 193

The Escorial 196
    Photographed by D. Anderson, Rome.

A rural mail-carrier 196

Machaquito — Spain's greatest bull-fighter . . 205

One of the Bombita family 205

"Aficionados del sol" 208

Peasants in Sunday best 208

A bread market 236

Market women 236

The Roman walls of Leon 244

View of Burgos from the Cerro de San Miguel . . 253

A donkey's siesta 253

Saintly generosity — Murillo 257
    Photographed by D. Anderson, Rome.

The land of the boina 260

Alfonso XIII at a picnic 260

A typical Spanish street 269

Wash-day 269

A guardia civil and an "aficionado" . . . 272

The baker makes his morning round . . . 272

FOUR MONTHS AFOOT IN SPAIN

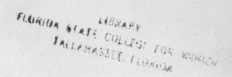

FOUR MONTHS AFOOT IN SPAIN

CHAPTER I

A 'TWEENDECKS JOURNEY

NOT the least of the virtues of the private schools
of New York City is the length of their summer vacations. It was an evening late in May
that I mounted to my lodgings in Hartley Hall,
rollicksome with the information that I should soon
be free from professional duties a full four months.
Where I preferred to spend that term of freedom
was easily decided. Except for one migratory
" year off," I had not been so long outside a class-
room since my fifth birthday; and it seemed fully
as far back that I had begun to dream of tramping
through Spain. If the desire had in earlier days
battened on mere curiosity, it found more rational
nourishment now in my hope of acquiring greater
fluency in the Spanish tongue, the teaching of which,
with other European languages, was the source of
my livelihood.

There was one potent obstacle, however, to my
jubilant planning. When I had set aside the small-

3

est portion of my savings that could tide me over
the first month of autumn, there was left a stark
one hundred and seventy-two dollars. The briefest
of mathematical calculations demonstrated that such
a sum could cover but scantily one hundred and
twenty days. Yet the blithesome project would not
be put to rout by mere figures. I had been well
schooled at least in the art of spending sparingly;
with a long summer before me I was not averse to
a bit of adventure, even the adventure of falling
penniless in foreign lands. A permanent stranding
was easily averted — I had but to leave in trust a
sum sufficient for repatriation, to be forwarded to
whatever corner of the globe insolvency might over-
haul me. Which, being done, I pocketed in express
checks and cash the remainder of my resources —
to-wit, one hundred and thirty-two dollars — tossed
into a battered suit-case a summer's supply of small
clothes and a thread-bare costume for ship wear, and
set out to discover what portion of the Iberian peninsula might be surveyed with such equipment.

Thus it was that on the morning of June first I
boarded the "L" as usual at One Hundred and
Sixteenth street; but took this time the west side
express instead of the local that screeches off at
Fifty-third into the heart of the city. A serge
suit of an earlier vintage and double-soled oxfords
were the chief articles of my attire, reduced already
to Spanish simplicity except for the fleckless collar

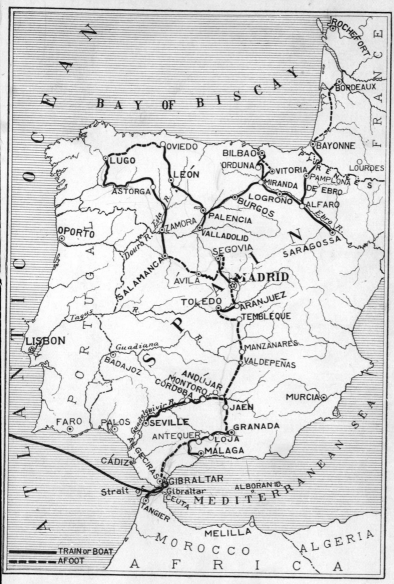

Showing the author's itinerary

and the cracked derby I had donned for the flight through exacting Manhattan. As for the suitcase that rocked against the platform gate as we roared southward, it was still far from a pedestrian's scrip. For with the ambitious resolution to rectify during the long sea voyage before me some of the sins of omission, I had stuffed into it at the last moment a dozen classic volumes in Sixth-avenue bindings.

" Christ 'fer ! " croaked the guard.

I descended to the street and threaded my way to the ferry. Across the river Hoboken was thronged with luggage-laden mankind, swarthy sons and daughters of toil for the most part; an eddying stream of which the general trend was toward a group of steamship docks. With it I was borne into a vast two-story pier, strewn below with everything that ships transport across the seas and resounding above with the voice of an excited multitude. Near the center of the upper wharf stood an isolated booth bearing a transient sign-board:

> " SCHNELLDAMPFER
> PRINZESSIN ———."

Within, sat a coatless, broad-gauge Teuton, puffing at a stogie.

" Third-class to Gibraltar," I requested, stooping to peer through the wicket.

The German reached mechanically for a pen and began to fill in a leaf of what looked like a large

check-book.   Then he paused and squinted out upon
me:

"Ah — er — you mean *steerage?* "

"Steerage, mein Herr; to Gibraltar."

He signed the blue check and pushed it toward
me, still holding it firmly by one corner.

"Thirty dollars and fifty cents," he rumbled.

I paid it and, ticket in hand, wormed my way
to the nearer of two gangways.   Here I was re-
pulsed; but at the second, an officer of immaculate
exterior but for two very bleary eyes, tore off a
corner of the blue check and jerked a thumb over
his shoulder toward the steamer behind him.   As I
set foot on her deck a seaman sprang up suddenly
from the scuppers and hurled at my chest a tightly
rolled blanket.   I caught it without a fumble, having
once dabbled in football, and, spreading it out on a
hatch, disclosed to view a deep tin plate, a huge
cup, a knife, fork and spoon of leaden hue, and a
red card announcing itself as "Buono per una
razione."

A hasty inspection of the *Prinzessin* ——— con-
firmed a suspicion that she would not offer the advantages of the steamers plying the northern route.
She was a princess indeed, a sailor's princess, such
as he may find who has the stomach to search in the
dives along West street or down on the lower
Bowery.   At her launching she had, perhaps, justi-
fied her christening; but long years have passed

since she was degraded to the unfastidious southern service.

The steerage section, congested now with disheveled Latins and cumbrous bundles, comprised the forward main deck, bounded on the bow by the forecastlehead and aft by an iron wall that rose a sheer eight feet to the first-class promenade, above which opened the hurricane deck and higher still the wheelhouse and bridge. This space was further limited by two large hatchways, covered with tarpaulins, of which a corner of each was thrown back to disclose two dark holes like the mouths of a mine. By these one entered the third-class quarters, of which the forward was assigned to " single men " and the other to any species of the human race that does not fall into that category. I descended the first by a perpendicular ladder to a dungeon where all but utter darkness reigned. As my eyes accustomed themselves to this condition, there grew up about me row after row of double-decked bunks, heaped with indistinct shapes. I approached the nearest and was confronted by two wolfish eyes, then another pair and another flashed up about me on every side. My foresighted fellow-passengers, having preëmpted sleeping-space, were prepared to hold their claims by force of arms — and baggage.

Every berth seemed to be taken. I meandered in and out among them until in a far corner I found one empty; but as I laid a hand upon its edge, a cadaverous youth sprang at me with a plaintive whine, " E mío! è mío! " I returned to the central space. A sweater-clad sailor whom I had not made out before was standing at the edge of an opening in the deck similar to that above.

" Qui non ch' è più," he said; " Giù! "

I descended accordingly to a second bridewell below the water-line and lighted only by a feeble electric bulb in the ceiling. Here half the bunks were unoccupied. I chose one athwartships against the forward bulkhead — a wooden bin containing a burlap sack of straw — tossed into it blanket and baggage, and climbed again to daylight and fresh air.

At eleven the sepulchral bass of the steamer sounded, the vast pier, banked with straining faces and fluttering handkerchiefs, began slowly to recede, sweeping with it the adjoining city, until all Hoboken had joined in the flight to the neighboring hills. We were off. I pitched overboard the cracked derby and crowded with a half-thousand others to the rail, eager for the long-anticipated pleasure of watching the inimitable panorama of New York grow smaller and smaller and melt away on the horizon. But we were barely abreast the Battery when three officers, alleging the impossibility of checking their human cargo on the open deck, ordered the entire steerage community below. When, long after, it came my turn to be released, my native land was utterly effaced, and the deck was spattering with a chilling rain before which we retreated and frittered away the remnant of the day with amical advances and bachelor banter.

In the morning the scene was transformed. Almost without exception my fellow-voyagers had changed from the somber garb of America to the picturesque comfort of their first landing in the western world. The steerage deck, flooded with sunshine, resembled the *piazza* of some Calabrian city on a day of festival. Women in many-hued vesture and brilliant *fazzoletti* sat in groups on the hatches, suckling their babes or mirthful over their knitting. Along the rail lounged men in bag-like trousers and tight-fitting jackets of velveteen, with broad scarlet sashes. Jaunty, deep-chested youths strolled fore and aft angling for glances from winsome eyes. Unromantic elders squatted in circles about the deck, screaming over games of *mora;* in and out among them all raced sportive *bambini.* High up on a winch sat a slender fellow Turkish fashion, thumbing a zither.

Though there was not one beside myself to whom that tongue was native, English was still the dominating language. Except for a handful of Greeks, the entire 'tweendecks company hailed from southern Italy or her islands. But force of habit or linguistic pride still gave full sway to the slang-strewn speech of east New York or the labor camp. There were not a few who might have expressed themselves far more clearly in some other medium, yet when I addressed them in Italian silence was frequently the response. The new world was still too close astern to give way to the spell of the old.

But it was in their mother tongue that I exchanged the first confidences with three young men with whom I passed many an hour during the journey. The mightiest was Antonio Massarone, a vociferous giant of twenty, whose scorn was unbounded for those of his race who had pursued fortune no further than the over-peopled cities of our eastern coast. Emigration had carried him to the mines of Nevada, and it was seldom that he refrained from patting his garnished waistband when tales of experience were exchanging. But the time had come when he must give up his princely wage of three dollars a day and return for years of drudgery and drill at as many cents, or forever forfeit the right to dwell in his native land. When his term was ended he would again turn westward; before that glad day comes what a stalwart task confronts certain officers of the Italian army!

Nicolò, too, expected to return. In fact, of all the steerage community a very few had resolved to remain at home, and for each of these there were a score who had emigrated a half-dozen times in the face of similar resolutions. Nicolò was a bootblack, proud of his calling and envious of no other. Already there hovered in his day dreams a three-chair

" parlor " in which his station should be nearest the
door and bordering on the cash-register. Conscription called him also, but he approached the day of
recruiting light of heart, knowing a man of four
feet nine would be quickly rejected.

As for Pietro Scerbo, the last of our quartet, his
home-coming was voluntary, for the family obligation
to the army had already been fulfilled by two older
brothers. Pietro had spent his eighteen months
kneading spaghetti dough in the Bronx at seven dollars a week; and he physically quaked at the sarcasm of 'Tonio on the subject of wages. Still he
was by no means returning empty-handed. " To be
sure, I am not rich with gold, like 'Tonio," he con-
fessed one day, when the miner was out of earshot,
" but I have spent only what I must — two dollars
in the boarding-house, sometimes some clothes, and
in the winter each week six lire to hear Caruso."

Thirty dollars a month and the peerless-voiced a
necessity of life! I, too, had been a frequent
" standee " at the Metropolitan, yet had as often
charged myself with being an extravagant young
rascal.

The steerage rations on the *Prinzessin* were in no
way out of keeping with her general unattractiveness.
Those who kept to their bunks until expelled by the
seaman whose duties included the daily fumigation
of the dungeons, were in no way the losers for being
deprived of the infantile roll and the strange imita-

tion of coffee that made up the European breakfast.
Sea breezes bring appetite, however, especially on a
faintly rippling ocean, and it was not strange that,
though the dinner-hour came early, even racial
lethargy fled at its announcement. Long before
noon a single jangle of the steward's bell cut short
all morning pastimes and instantly choked the passages to the lower regions with a clamorous, jocose
struggle of humanity as those on deck dived below
for their meal-hour implements and collided with the
foresighted, fighting their way up the ladders.
Once disentangled, we filed by the mouth of the
culinary cavern under the forecastlehead, to receive each a ladleful of the particular pièce de ré-
sistance of the day, a half-grown loaf of bread, and
a brimming cupful of red wine. Thus laden, each
squirmed his way through the multitude and made
table of whatever space offered,— on the edge of a
hatch, the drum of a winch, or on the deck itself.

Unvaryingly day by day boiled beef alternated with
pork and beans. Then there was macaroni, not alternately, nor yet moderately, but ubiquitously,
fourteen days a week; for supper was in no way
different from dinner even in the unearthly hour of its
serving. It was tolerably coarse macaroni, but
otherwise no worse than omnipresent macaroni must
be when boiled by the barrel under the watchful eye
of a rotund, torpescent, bath-fearing, tobacco-loving,
Neapolitan ship's cook. For the wine we were

A street in terraced Gibraltar

supremely grateful; not that it was particularly good wine, but such as it was not even the pirates in the galley could make it worse.

The ensembled climax of this daily extravaganza, however, had for its setting the steerage "wash-room," an iron cell furnished with two asthmatic salt-water faucets. To it dashed first the long experienced in the quick-lunch world, and on their heels the competing multitude. The 'tweendecks strongholds housed six hundred, the "wash-room" six, whence it goes without saying that the minority was always in power and the majority howling for admittance and a division of the spoils. Yet dissension, as is wont, was rampant even among the sovereign. From within sounded the splashing of water, the tittering of jostled damsels, or the shouting for passage of one who had resigned his post and must run the gauntlet to freedom through a vociferous raillery. In due time complete rotation in office was accomplished, but it was ever a late hour when the last gourmand emerged from the alleyway and carried his dripping utensils below.

The *Prinzessin* plowed steadily eastward. Gradually, as the scent of the old world came stronger to our nostrils, the tongue of the West fell into disuse. Had I been innocent of Italian I must soon have lost all share in the general activities. As it was, I had the entrée to each group; even the solemn socialists, seated together behind the winch planning the details of the portending reversal of society, did not lower their voices as I passed.

How little akin are anticipation and realization! Ever before on the high seas it had been my part to labor unceasingly among cattle pens or to bear the moil of watch and watch; and the unlimited leisure of the ticketed had seemed always fit object for envy. Yet here was I myself at last crossing the Atlantic as a passenger, and weary already of this forced inactivity before the voyage was well begun. The first full day, to be sure, had passed delightfully, dozing care-free in the sun or striding through the top-most volume in my luggage. But before the second was ended reading became a bore; idling more fatiguing than the wielding of a coal-shovel. On the third, I sauntered down into the forecastle more than half inclined to suggest to one of its inmates a reversal of rôles; but the watch below greeted me with that chill disdain accorded mere passengers, never once lapsing into the masculine banter that would have marked my acceptance as an equal. As a last resort I set off on long pedestrian tours of the deck, to the astonishment of the lounging Latins, though now and then some youth inoculated with the restlessness of the West, notably 'Tonio, fell in with me for a mile or two.

It was the miner, too, who first accepted my challenge to a bout of hand-wrestling and quickly brought me undeserved fame by sprawling prone on his back, when, had he employed a tithe of science, he might have tossed me into the scuppers. From the moment of its introduction this exotic pastime won great popularity. Preliminary jousts filled the morning hours; toward evening the hatches were transformed into grandstands from which the assembled third-class populace cheered on the panting contestants and greeted each downfall with a cannonade of laughter, in which even the vanquished joined.

More constant and universal than all else, however, was the demand for music. The most diffident possessor of a mouth-organ or a jew's-harp knew no peace during his waking hours. Great was the joy when, as dusk was falling on the second day out, a Calabrian who had won fortune and corpulence as a grocer in Harlem, clambered on deck, straining affectionately to his bosom a black box with megaphone attachment.

" E un fonógrafo," he announced proudly; " a present I take to the old madre at home." He warded off with his elbows the exultant uprising and deposited the instrument tenderly on a handkerchief spread by his wife on a corner of the hatch. " For a hundred dollars, signori! " he cried; " Madre di Dío! How she will wonder if there is a little man in the box! For on the first day, signori, I do not tell her how the music is put in the fonógrafo, ha! ha! ha! not for a whole day! "— and the joke came perilously near to choking him into apoplexy long before its perpetration.

A turn of the key and the apparatus struck up "La donna è móbile," the strikingly clear tones floating away on the evening air to blend with the wash of the sea on our bow. A hush fell over the forward deck; into the circle of faces illumed by the swinging ship's lantern crept the mirage of dreams; a sigh sounded in the black night of the outskirts.

" E Bonci, amici," whispered the Calabrian as the last note died away.

The announcement was superfluous; no one else could have sung the sprightly little lyric with such perfection.

Bits of other operas followed, plantation melodies, and the monologues of witty Irishmen; but always the catholic instrument came back to " La donna è móbile," and one could lean back on one's elbows and fancy the dapper little tenor standing in person on the corner of the hatch, pouring out his voice to his own appreciative people.

Thereafter as regularly as the twilight appeared the Calabrian with his " fonógrafo." The forward deck took to sleeping by day that the evening musicale might be prolonged into the small hours. Whatever its imperfections, the little black box did much to charm away the monotony of the voyage, in its early stages.

But good fortune is rarely perennial. One night

in mid-Atlantic a first-class passenger of the type
that adds, by contrast, to the attractiveness of the
steerage, his arms about the waists of two damsels
old enough to have known better, paused to hang
over the rail. Bonci was singing. The promenader
surveyed the oblivious multitude below in silence until
the aria ended, then turned on his heel with a snort
of contempt. The maidens giggled, the affectionate
trio strolled aft, and a moment later the cabin
piano was jangling a Broadway favorite. When I
turned my head the Calabrian was closing his instrument.

"No, amici, no more," he said as protest rose;
"We must not annoy the rich signori up there."

Nor could he be moved to open the apparatus
again as long as the voyage lasted.

Amid the general merriment of home-coming was
here and there a note of sadness in the caverns of
the *Prinzessin*. On a hatch huddled day by day, when
the sun was high, a family of three, doomed to early
extinction by the white-faced scourge of the north.
Below, it was whispered, lay an actress once famous
in the Italian quarter, matched in a race with death
to her native village. A toil-worn Athenian, on
life's down grade, who had been robbed on the very
eve of sailing of seven years' earnings of pick and
shovel, tramped the deck from dawn to midnight
with sunken head, refusing either food or drink.
Now and again he stepped to the rail to shake his

2

knotted fist at the western horizon, stretched his arms on high, and took up again his endless march.

Then there were the deported — seven men whose berths were not far from my own. One had shown symptoms of trachoma; another bore the mark of a bullet through one hand; a third was a very Hercules, whom the port doctors had pronounced flawless, but who had landed with four dollars less than the twenty-five required. With this single exception, however, one could not but praise the judgment of Ellis Island. The remaining four were dwarfish Neapolitans, little more than wharf rats; and the best of Naples bring little that is desirable. Yet one could not but pity the unpleasing little wretches, who had risen so far above their environment as to save money in a place where money is bought dearly, and whose only reward for years of repression of every appetite had been a month of misery and frustration.

"Porca di Madonna!" cursed the nearest, pointing to three small blue scars on his neck; "For nothing but these your infernal doctors have made me a beggar!"

"On the sea, when it was too late," whined his companion, "they told me we with red eyes should not go to New York, but to a city named Canada. Madre dí Dío! Why did I not take my ticket to this Canada?"

"You will next time?" I hinted.

"Next time!" he shrieked, dropping from his bunk as noiselessly as a cat. "Is there a *next time* with a book like that?" He shook in my face the libretto containing a record of his activities since birth, lacking which no Italian of the proletariat may live in peace in his own land nor embark for another. Across every page was stamped indelibly the word "deported."

"They ruined it, curse them! It's something in your maledetta American language that tells the police not to let me go and the agenzia not to sell me a ticket. My book is destroyed! Sono scomunicato! And where shall I get the money for this next time, díceme? To come to America I have worked nine, ten, sangue della Vergine! how do I know how many years! Why did I not take the ticket to this Canada?"

On the morning of June seventh we raised the Azores; at first the dimmest blot on the horizon, a point or two off the starboard bow, as if the edge of heaven had been salt-splashed by a turbulent wave. Excited dispute arose in the throng that quickly mustered at the rail. All but the nautical-eyed saw only a cloud, which in a twinkling the hysterical had pronounced the forerunner of a howling tempest that was soon to bring to the *Prinzessin* the dreaded *mal di mare*, perhaps even ununctioned destruction.

One quaking father drove his family below and barricaded his corner against the tornado-lashed night to come.

An hour brought reassurance, however, and with it jubilation as the outpost of the eastern world took on corporate form. Before sunset we were abreast the island. An oblong hillside sloped upward to a cloud-cowled peak. Villages rambled away up tortuous valleys; here and there the green was dotted with chalk-white houses and whiter churches. Higher still the island was mottled with duodecimo fields of grain, each maturing in its own season; while far and near brilliant red windmills, less stolid and thick-set than those of Holland, toiled in the breeze, not hurriedly but with a deliberate vivacity befitting the Latin south. Most striking of all was a scent of profoundest peace that came even to the passing ship, and a suggestion of eternal summer, not of burning days and sultry nights, but of early June in some fairy realm utterly undisturbed by the clamorous rumble of the outer world.

Two smaller islands appeared before the day was done, one to port so near that we could count the cottage windows and all but make out the features of skirt-blown peasant women standing firm-footed in deep green meadows against a background of dimming hills. As the night descended, the houses faded to twinkling lights, now in clusters, now a

stone's-throw one from another, but not once failing
as long as we remained on deck.

For two days following the horizon was unbroken.
Then through the morning mists of June tenth rose
Cabo San Vicente, the scowling granite corner-stone
of Europe, every line of its time-scarred features a
defiance to the sea and a menace to the passerby.
Beyond stretched a wrinkled, verdureless plateau,
to all appearances unpeopled, and falling into the
Atlantic in grim, oxide-stained cliffs that here advanced within hailing distance, there retreated to
the hazy horizon. All through the day the world's
commerce filed past,— water-logged tramps crawling along the face of the land, whale-like oil tanks
showing only a dorsal fin of funnel and deck-house,
East Indiamen straining Biscayward, and all the
smaller fry of fishermen and coasters. A rumor,
rising no one knew where, promised that early morning should find us entering the Mediterranean. I
subsidized the services of a fellow-voyager dexterous
with shears and razor and, reduced to a tuft of fore-
lock, descended once more to the lower dungeon.

Long before daylight I was awakened by the
commissario, or steerage steward, tugging at a leg
of my trousers and screeching in his boyish falsetto,
" Gibiltèrra! Make ready! Gibiltèrra! " It was
no part of the commissario's duties to call third-
class passengers. But ever since the day he had

examined my ticket, the little whisp of a man who never ceased to regard me with suspicion, as if he doubted the sanity of a traveler who was bound for a land that was neither Italy nor America. Of late he seemed convinced that my professed plan was merely a ruse to reach Naples without paying full fare, and he eyed me askance now as I clambered from my bunk, in his pigwidgeon face a stern determination that my knavery should not succeed.

Supplied with a bucket by a sailor, I climbed on deck and approached the galley. The cook was snoring in a corner of his domain; his understudy was nowhere to be seen. I tip-toed to the hot-water faucet and was soon below again stripping off my " ship's clothes," which the obliging seaman, having bespoken this reward, caught up one by one as they fell. The splashing of water aroused the encircling sleepers. Gradually they slid to the deck and gathered around me, inquiring the details of my eccentric plan. By the time I was dressed in the best my suitcase offered, every mortal in the " single " quarters had come at least once to bid me a dubious farewell.

The commissario returned and led the way in silence along the deserted promenade to the deck abaft the cabins. The *Prinzessin* lay at anchor. A half-mile away, across a placid lagoon, towered the haggard Rock of Gibraltar, a stone-faced city strewn along its base. About the harbor, glinting

in the slanting sunlight, prowled rowboats, sloops,
and yawls, and sharp-nosed launches. One of the
latter soon swung in against the starboard ladder
and there stepped on deck two men in white uniforms, who seated themselves without a word at a
table which the commissario produced by some magic
of his own, and fell to spreading out impressive docu-
ments. A glance sufficed to recognize them English-
men. At length the older raised his head with an
interrogatory jerk, and the commissario, with the
air of a man taken red-handed in some rascality,
minced forward and laid on the table a great legal
blank with one line scrawled across it.

"T'ird classy maneefesto, signori," he apologized.

"Eh!" cried the Englishman. "A steerage passenger for Gibraltar?"

The steward jerked his head backward toward me.

"Humph!" said the spokesman, inspecting me
from crown to toe. "Where do you hail from?"

Before I could reply there swarmed down the com-
panionway a host of cabin passengers, in port-of-
call array, whom the Englishman greeted with bared
head and his broadest welcome-to-our-city smile;
then bowed to the launch ladder. As he resumed his
chair I laid my passport before him.

"For what purpose do you desire to land in
Gibraltar?" he demanded.

"I am bound for Spain—" I began.

" Spain ! " shouted the Briton, with such emphasis
as if that land lay at the far ends of the earth.
" Indeed! Where are you going from Gibraltar,
and how soon? "

" Until I get ashore I can hardly say; in a day or
so, at least; to Granada, perhaps, or Málaga."

" Out of respect for the American passport," replied the Englishman grandiloquently, " I am
going to let you land. But see you stick to this
story."

I descended to the launch and ten minutes later
landed with my haughty fellow-tourists at a bawling,
tout-lined wharf. An officer peeped into my hand-
bag, and I sauntered on through a fortress gate
under which a sun-scorched Tommy Atkins marched
unremittingly to and fro. Beyond, opened a narrow street, paralleling the harbor front and peopled
even at this early hour with a mingling of races that
gave to the scene the aspect of a temperate India, or
a scoured and rebuilt Egypt. Sturdy British
troopers in snug khaki and roof-like tropical hel-
mets strode past; bare-legged Moors in flowing
bournous stalked by in the widening streak of sunshine along the western walls; the tinkle of goat-bells
mingled with the rhythmic cries of their drivers,
offering a cup fresh-drawn to whomever possessed
a copper; now an orange woman hobbled by, chanting her wares; everywhere flitted swarthy little men
in misfit rags, with small baskets of immense straw-

berries which sold for a song to all but the tourists
who tailed out behind me.

Suddenly, a furlong beyond the gate, a sign-
board flashed down upon me, and I turned instinc-
tively in at the open door of the "Seaman's
Institute." I found myself in a sort of restaurant,
with here and there a pair of England's soldiers at
table, and a towsled youth of darker tint hanging
over the bar. I commanded ham and eggs; when
they were served the youth dropped into the chair
opposite and, leaning on his elbows, smiled speechlessly upon me, as if the sight of an unfamiliar face
brought him extraordinary pleasure.

"Room to put me up?" I asked.

"Nothin' much else but room," sighed the youth,
in the slurring speech of the Anglo-Spanish half-
cast, "but the super's not up yet, an' I'm only
the skittles."

I left my baggage in his keeping and, roaming
on through the rapidly warming city to the Alameda
Gardens, clambered away the day on the blistered
face of the great Rock above.

The "super," a flabby-muscled tank of an Englishman, was lolling out the evening among his cli-
ents when I reëntered the Institute. My request
for lodging roused him but momentarily from his
lethargy.

"Sign off here?" he drawled.

"Left the *Prinzessin* this morning," I answered,

suddenly reminded that I was no longer a seaman prepared to produce my discharge-book on demand.

" A.B., eh? "

" Been before the mast on the *Warwickshire*, *Glen*—"

" All right. A bob a night is our tax. But no smoking aloft," he added, as I dropped a coin on the table before him.

" 'Ow ye like Gib? " asked the half-cast, leading the way up a narrow stairway.

" Like it," I replied.

" Yes, they all does," he mourned, " for one day. But 'ow if you 'ad always to bask on the stewin' old Rock, like a bally lizard? Saint Patrick! If only some toff 'ud pay me a ticket to America! "

He entered a great room, divided by thin wooden partitions into a score of small ones, and, tramping down a hallway, lighted me into the last chamber. Opposite the cot was a tall window with heavy wooden blinds. I flung them open and leaned out over the *reja;* and all at once, unheralded, the Spain of my dreams leaped into reality. Below, to one side, flowed the murmuring stream of Gibraltar's main thoroughfare; further away the flat-roofed city descended in moonlit indistinctness into the Mediterranean. From a high-walled garden a pebble-toss away and canopied with fragrant fruit-trees, rose the twang of a guitar and a man's clear voice singing a languorous air of Andalusia. Now and

again a peal of laughter broke on the night and
drifted away on the wings of the indolent sea-breeze.
I rolled a cigarette and lighted it pensively, not in
contempt for the " super's " orders, but because
some transgression of established law seemed the
only fitting celebration of the untrammeled summer
that was opening before me.

CHAPTER II

GIBRALTAR rises early. Proof of the assertion may be lacking, but certainly not even a "Rock lizard" could recompose himself for another nap after the passing of the crashing military band that snatched me at daybreak back to the waking world. With one bound I sprang from cot to window. But there was no ground for alarm; in gorge-like Waterport street below, Thomas Atkins, a regiment strong, was marching briskly barrackward, sweeping the flotsam of civilian life into the nooks and crannies of the flanking buildings.

According to the Hoyle of travelers a glimpse of Morocco was next in order. But with the absurdity of things inanimate and Oriental both the Tangiers steamers were scheduled to loll out the day in harbor. When "Skittles" had again stowed away my chattels, I drifted aimlessly out into the city. But the old eagerness to tread Spanish soil was soon upon me, heightened now by the sight of Algeciras gleaming across the bay. The harbor steamer would have landed me there a mere peseta poorer. Instead, I sauntered through the Landport gate and away along the shifting highway which the Holder of the Rock has dubbed, in his insular tongue, the " Road to Spain."

It led me past the double rank of sentry boxes between which soldiers of England tramp everlastingly, and into bandit-famed La Linea. A Spaniard in rumpled uniform scowled out upon me from the first stone hovel, but, finding me empty-handed, as silently withdrew. I turned westward through the disjointed town and out upon the curving shore of the bay.

Here was neither highway nor path. Indeed, were each Spanish minute tagged with a Broadway pricemark, the peseta would have been dearly saved, for the apparent proximity of Algeciras had been but a tricking of the eye. Hour after hour I waded on through seashore sand, halting now and then in the shadow of some time-gnawed watch-tower of the departed Moor, before me such a survey of the shimmering sea to the very base of the hazy African coast as amply to justify the setting of an outlook on this jutting headland.

The modern guardian of the coast dwells more lowly. Every here and there I came upon a bleached and tattered grass hut just out of reach of the languid surf, and under it a no less ragged and listless *carabinero* squatted in Arabic pose and tranquillity, musket within reach, or frankly and audibly asleep on his back in the sand. Yet his station, too, was

wisely chosen. The watch and ward of to-day is set
for no war-trimmed galley from the rival continent,
but against petty smugglers skulking along the rim
of the bay. Nor could the guard better spend his
day than asleep: his work falls at night.

It was the hour of *siesta* when I shuffled up a
sandy bank into Algeciras. Except for a cur or two
that slunk with wilted tail across the *plaza*, the town
lay in sultry repose. I sat down in a shaded corner
of the square. Above me nodded the aged city tower,
housing the far-famed and often-cursed bell of
Algeciras. Recently, which is to say some time during the past century, it was cracked from rim to
crown; and the city fathers have not yet taken up
the question of its replacement. Meanwhile, it con-
tinues afflictingly faithful to its task. At quarter-
hourly intervals it clanked out across the bay like the
suspended hull of a battleship beaten with the butt
of a cannon, a languid sigh rose over the drowsing
city, and silence settled down anew.

As the shadows spread, life revived, slowly and
yawningly at first, then swelling to a contrasting
merry-making that reached its climax toward midnight in the festooned streets beyond the plaza.
Algeciras was celebrating her annual *feria*. Somewhere I fell in with a carpenter in blouse and hemp
sandals, whose Spanish flowed musically as a wood-
land brook, and together we sauntered out the
evening among the lighted booths. The amusement

mongers were toiling lustily. Gypsy and clown, *bolerina*, juggler, and ballad-singer drew each his little knot of idlers, but a multitude was massed only around the gambling tables. Here a hubbub of excited voices assailed the ear; an incessant rain of coins fell on the green cloth, from the ragged and the tailored, from quavering crones and little children. The carpenter dived into the fray with his only peseta, screaming with excitement as the wheel stopped on the number he had played. Within an hour a pocket of his blouse was bulging with silver. I caught him by the sleeve and shouted a word in his ear. Wild horses could not have dragged him away, nor the voices of sirens have distracted his eyes from the spinning trundle. A half-hour later he did not possess a copper.

"If you had listened," I said, when we had reached a conversational distance, "you would not have lost your fortune."

"What fortune!" he panted. "All I have lost, señor, is one peseta, and had an evening of a lifetime."

I caught the morning steamer to Gibraltar and an hour later was pitching across the neck of the Mediterranean on board the *Gebel Dersa*. Third-class fare to Africa was one peseta; first-class, ten; and the difference in accommodation about forty feet,— to wit, the distance from the forward to the after-deck. One peseta, indeed, seemed to be the fixed

charge for any service in this corner of the world.
My evening meal, the night's lodging, the boatman's
fee for setting me aboard the steamer had each cost
as much. It would be as easy to quote a fixed selling-
price for mining-stocks as to set the value of that
delusive Spanish coin. The summer's average, however, was close upon sixteen cents for the peseta, of
which the *céntimo* is the hundredth part. There are
at large, be it further noted, a vast number of home-
made pesetas worth just sixteen cents less, which
show great affinity for the stranger's pocket until
such time as he learns to emulate the native and sound
each coin on the stone set into every counter.

It was while we were skirting the calcined town of
Tarifa that I made the acquaintance of Aghmed
Shat. The introduction was not of my seeking —
but of the ingratiating ways of Aghmed I need say
nothing, known as he is by every resident of our
land. At least I can recall no fellow-countryman
whose visiting-card he did not dig up from the
abysmal confusion of his inner garments.

To that host of admirers it will bring grief to
learn that Aghmed was most unjustly treated aboard
the *Gebel Dersa* on that blistering thirteenth day of
June. Yet facts must be reported. It chanced that
the dozen Anglo-Saxons sprawled ungracefully
about the after-deck composed, at such times as
composure was possible, a single party. As all the
world knows, it is for no other purpose than to

"The Road to Spr..."

offer the protection of his name and learning to just such defenseless flocks that the high-born Moroccan gentleman in question has been journeying thrice weekly to the Rock these thirty years. Yet the bell-wether of the party, blind to his opportunity, had chosen as guide an ignorant, vile, ugly, utterly un-principled rascal whose only motive was mercenary. True, Aghmed and the rascal were outwardly as alike as two bogus pesetas. But surely any man worthy the title of personal conductor should be versed in the reading of character, or at least able to distinguish between genuine testimonials from the world's élite and a parcel of bald forgeries! Worst of all, the leader, with that stiff-neckedness con-genital to his race, had persisted in his error even after Aghmed had recounted in full detail the rascal's crimes. Small wonder there was dejection in the face of the universally-recommended as he crossed the pitching plank that connected the first-class with the baser world, his skirts threshing in the wind, his turban awry.

At sight of me, however, he brightened visibly. With outstretched hand and a wan smile he minuetted forward and seated himself on the hatch beside me with the unobtrusive greeting:

" Why for you travel third-class? "

The question struck me as superfluous. But it is as impossible to scowl down Aghmed's spirit of in-vestigation as to stare him into believing an Amer-

3

ican a Spaniard. By the time the valleys of the
African coast had begun to take on individuality, I
had heard not only the full story of his benevolent
life but had refused for the twentieth time his disin-
terested offer of protection. Nature, however, made
Aghmed a guardian of his fellow-man, as she has
made other hapless mortals poets; and her commands
must be carried out at whatever sacrifice. Gradually,
slowly, sadly, the "souvenir" which "americano
gentlemen" were accustomed to bestow upon him
with their farewell hand-clasp fell from twenty shil-
lings to ten, to five, to three, then to as many pesetas.
It was useless to explain that I had trusted to my
own guidance in many an Arab land, and been fully
satisfied with the service. When every other argu-
ment had fallen lifeless at his slippered feet, he sent
forth at regular intervals the sole survivor, cheering
it on with a cloud of acrid cigarette smoke:

"Si el señor"—for his hamstrung English had
not far endured the journey—"if the gentleman has
never taken a guide, this will be a new experience."

In the end the sole survivor won. What, after all,
is travel but a seeking after new experience? Here,
in truth, was one; and I might find out for myself
whether a full-grown man tagging through the
streets of a foreign city on the heels of a twaddle-
spouting native feels as ridiculous as he looks.

We anchored toward noon in the churning harbor
of Tangiers and were soon pitched into the pande-

monium of all that goes to make up an Oriental mob '
lying in wait for touring Europeans. In a twinkling, Aghmed had engaged donkeys to carry us to
the principal hotel. I paused on the outskirts of
the riot to inform him that our sight-seeing would
be afoot; and with a scream of astonishment he reeled
and would, perhaps, have fallen had not the street
been paved in that which would have made such stage-
business unpleasant.

"Pero, señor!" he gasped. "You do not — you
— why, people will say you have no money!"

"Horrible!" I cried, dodging a slaughtered sheep
on the head of a black urchin in scanty night-shirt
that dashed suddenly out of a slit between two buildings. Aghmed, myopic with excitement, failed to
side-step, and it was some distance beyond that his
wail again fell on my ear:

"O señor! Americano gentlemen never go by this
street. I cannot guide without donkeys —"

"You can perhaps run along home to dinner?" I
suggested; but he merely fell silent and pattered on
at my heels, now and again heaving a plaintive sigh.

For the better part of the day we roamed in and
out through the tangled city. In the confusion of
donkeys, bare legs, and immodesty, the narcotic
smell of hashish, the sound of the harsh guttural
tongue once so familiar, memories of more distant
Mohammedan lands surged upon me. Yet by comparison Tangiers seemed only a faded segment of

the swarming Arab world set aside to overawe European tourists, Arabic enough in its way, but only a little, mild-mannered sample.

Late in the afternoon I rounded the beach and, falling upon the highway to Fez, strolled away out of sight and sound of the seaport. Aghmed still languished at my heels. To him also the day had brought a new experience. As we leaned back against a grassy slope to watch the setting of the red sun, he broke a long hour's silence.

" Señor," he said, " never have I walked so much. When we had come to the Socco I was tired. When we had seen all the city my legs were as two stone pillars. Yet I must keep walking."

" Why? " I asked.

" Because you must be protected! Ah, señor, you do not know how dangerous is Tangiers; and here in the country alone you would before now be dead, or carried off by bandits. Perhaps this much walking will make me sick. Or if I have been seen by my friends or a gentleman tourist! Allah meskeen! They will say I am no longer a gentleman guide, but a donkey boy."

When her night traffic had taken on its wonted swing, my stone-legged protector called at the inn for the purpose of proving that the far-famed naughtiness of his city was no mere conceit. The demonstration was not convincing. Two hours or more we ambled from wineshop to *café cantante*, en-

during a deal of caterwauling and inane vulgarity
by no means superior to a Friday-night performance
on the Bowery. The relieving shepherd's crook,
moreover, being nowhere in evidence, I fled the torture and retired to bed.

To my infinite relief, Aghmed was on hand in full
health next morning to bid me farewell at the end
of the pier and to receive his specified " souvenir."
He was profuse, too, with the hope that I might soon
revisit his land; but I caught no hint of a desire to
add my card to his collection.

The steamer plowed her way back to Europe, and
by mid-afternoon I emerged from the Sailor's Institute face to face with a serious problem. The most
patient of men, which I am not, would hardly set off
on a tramp across the Iberian peninsula carrying a
forty-pound suitcase, even of unread classics. To
have dumped the books in the first alleyway would
have been easy, yet painful, for there runs a strain
of Scotch in my veins. I dropped in on the nearest
bookseller to inquire whether he could see his way
clear to accept at a bargain a batch of novels newly
imported from New York. But the eager glow
quickly faded from his features as I laid the volumes
before him.

" Why, sir! " he cried. " These be *old* books, out
of date. I thought had you something New York
is reading this summer —"

In which attitude his two rivals also dismissed me,

even though I sought the good will of the last by squandering the bulk of a bright gold sovereign for Baedeker's " Spain." As I turned down to the harbor, a thought, or more exactly the sight of a sergeant's uniform under the fortress gate, struck me. The wearer stiffened like a ramrod when I halted before him.

" Have you a library in the barracks? "

" Ah — certainly, garrison library. But I hardly fawncy the commander would allow —"

" Of course not," I interrupted, tossing the books into his arms; " but I am off for Spain and if you have any use for a few novels —"

" Ah — er — well, thank you most kindly, sir!" bawled the officer after me.

Though the fact may never be called to his attention, the sergeant had heard the last phrase of English that passed my lips in many a week. As a personal experiment I had resolved not to speak a word of my native tongue within the kingdom of Spain, even to myself; though this latter proviso, to be sure, necessitated the early acquisition of a few Spanish terms of double voltage.

The forerunner of evening was descending upon Algeciras as I mounted through her now all but voiceless fiesta and struck away over a grass-patched hillock. The further slope was skirted by a dusty highway that wound off through a billowy country pregnant with the promise of greater heights to

come. But the trend of the road was west rather
than north. Over the hills ahead two male voices
were bawling a sort of dialogue of song. I mended
my pace and had soon overtaken two peasants rol-
licking homeward from the festival. When I inquired
if this were the highway to Madrid they fell suddenly
silent, after a word of greeting, and strode along beside me exchanging puzzled glances.

"Well, then, to Ronda, señores?" I asked. "Por
esta carretera?"

"No, no, señor!" they answered quickly. "Por
aquí no! You must go on the railroad."

"No, I am traveling on foot."

"Perfectamente, señor; and to walk to Ronda you
must take the railroad."

There was nothing in the mien of either to suggest
the practical joker. Yet so far as my experience
carried there was not a corner of Europe where two
steps on the right of way was rated less a crime than
arson or housebreaking.

We reached the line not far beyond, the highway
diving under by a stone-faced cutting and bearing the
peasants away with it. Over the next rise their dove-
tailed duet rang out again and, melting in volume
and rendered almost musical by distance, filtered back
to me from the deepening valleys a full quarter-hour
longer.

I climbed the embankment not without misgiving.
Sure enough, a track there was, beside the broad-

gauge rails, covered with cinders and scarred with many imprints of donkey hoofs. A mile along it demonstrated how poor a walking kit is even a half-empty suitcase. I sat down to take stock of the contents. In the jumble was a blue flannel shirt past its prime. I fished out thread and needle and sewed a Jack-Tar seam across the garment below the armpits, amputated sleeves and shoulders with a few slashes, and behold! a knapsack that might bear my burdens through all the kingdom of Spain, and hold its own in any gathering of shoulder-packed wayfarers. When I had stuffed my possessions into it there was still room to spare for such odds and ends as find their way into the baggage of the least acquisitive of travelers. Then pitching the suitcase spread-eagle over the bordering hedge, I cut a stick in a neighboring thicket and struck off again at the regular stride so indispensable to any true enjoyment of tramping.

Night fell soon after. A fall it was indeed; no half-hearted settling down of gloom as in our northern zone, but a descendant flood of obscurity that left the eyes blinking in dismay. To right and left, where had been rolling uplands and heathered fields sharp-cut in smallest detail, nothing — a sea of inky blackness; and ahead, the stony-blind unknown. The cinder path held firm, but only a foot rubbing along the rail guided my steps, until such time as sight resumed its leadership.

An hour or more I marched on into the summer night. Then out of the darkness ahead stole a feeble point of light, an increasing murmur of human voices, and the end of the first day's tramp was before me. Beside the way a stone building stood open, an oil torch twilighting a cobble-floored room heaped at one end with a Spanish grocer's wares. An unshaven man of fifty, a red handkerchief bound brigand-fashion about his head, bulked forward through an inner doorway.

" You furnish lodgings? "

" Sí, señor; and your burro? "

" I am walking. Is supper to be had? "

" Claro, hombre! Choose from the baskets and the señora shall cook it for you in a twinkling."

All through the following day the path continued parasitic to the railway. The roadbed was thickly covered with crushed stone, with nowhere a hint of the existence of section-gangs. On either hand rolled away a landscape stamped with the features of an African ancestry, all but concealed at times by the cactus-trees of a willow's height that hedged the track. At rare intervals a stuccoed station serving some hamlet hidden among the hills found standing-room on the right of way. An occasional hovel built of field stones frowned down from the crest of a parched hillock. Now and again out of the meeting-place of the rails ahead came jogging a peasant seated sidewise on an ass, to swerve suddenly aside and rattle off down a rocky gorge, singing a high-pitched ballad of Arabic cadence. But these were but bubbles on the surface of a fathomless solitude, though a solitude brilliant with an all-invading sunshine that left no skulking-place for somber moods.

It turned out that the railroad had not been built for the exclusive convenience of pedestrians and donkeys. A bit before noon a rumbling arose out of the north, and no unconscionable time thereafter the daily " expreso " roared by — at a rate close upon fifteen miles an hour. The ticket collector, cigarette in mouth, clambered hand over hand along the running board, in imminent peril of losing his footing — and being obliged to pursue his train to the next station. During the afternoon there passed two " mixtos," toy freight trains with a caudal carload of passengers. But the speed of these was more reasonable, varying from six to eight miles, with vacations at each station and frequent holidays in the open country.

The sun was still an hour high when I reached the station of San Pablo. This time the town itself stood in plain sight, pitched on the summit of an oak-grown hill barely a mile from the line. I plunged quickly down into the intervening valley.

It was a checker-board place, perhaps only a century or two old; certainly no relic of the Moor, for there was not a sign of shop or market in all its extent. Only in the last street did I catch sight of one of its inhabitants, dining in solitary state in the center of a bare room. He stared at me a long moment when I halted before the immense open window to inquire for an inn.

"San Pablo, señor," he answered at last, "is a private town owned by the mining company. There is no inn."

I was turning away when he continued:

"But step inside and we shall see what the ama can arrange for you."

He was, as I had guessed, a Frenchman, an expert employed in the mines. The Spanish, however, in which he addressed the *ama* was faultless.

"Ah, Don Victor!" protested that matron, "How can I give posada, having no license from the government? And without the permission of Don José —"

"Pepete," said the Gaul to an urchin peering in upon us, "ask Don José to have the goodness to step over. He is manager of the mines," he continued, "and so alcalde and potentate of San Pablo."

It would have been a misfortune, indeed, to have journeyed through Andalusia without making the acquaintance of Don José. He burst in upon us a moment later; a very hippopotamus of a man, dressed in baggy trousers, slouch hat, and alpaca jacket. Unfortunately his arrival coincided with my announcement that I was walking to Córdoba — the whole itinerary would have been too strong meat for Latin consumption — and his native geniality was for a time overshadowed by astonishment at my extraordinary means of locomotion. I had all but finished the meal set for me in an adjoining room when the pair entered and sat down beside me.

" Señor," began the manager, in what was meant to be a whisper, " you cannot walk to Córdoba. It is forty leagues."

" How much money have you? " put in the Frenchman.

" Er — I have something over seven pesetas," I answered.

" Bueno! Bonísima! " cried the alcalde, patting me on the shoulder. " Don Victor and I will add the rest and I shall go with you to the station to buy the ticket — in the morning."

Great, I reflected, is the infant mortality among generous resolutions in the gray of dawn, and accordingly held my peace.

Having settled my future to his own satisfaction, Don José linked an arm in one of mine and plunged out into the night.

" Your bed is waiting for you in your own house," he said with Spanish formality. " You have only to say the word."

The first syllable of which I had not found time to say before we marched full front into San Pablo's barrack-like café. A roar of greeting sounded through the dense cloud of cigarette smoke: " Buenas tardes! Don José! "

"Buenas, amigos! Que le gusta!" returned my companion, and pushing toward a table with two vacant chairs he continued without a break, "Un ponche, Don Gregario! And you, señor? Anything you may choose, though there is nothing equal to ponche. Verdad, Rufo?" Then as I opened my lips to express a preference, "Sí! sí! Don Gregario! Dos ponches!"

The room was filled with a hundred bronze-tinted miners over wine and cards. Don José was the industrial autocrat of every man present, yet one would have fancied him rather a brother or cousin, so free was the intercourse from haughtiness on the one hand and servility on the other. Miner and manager addressed each other by their given names, shouted at each other in friendly dispute, thumped each other fraternally on the back. Despite all which one felt absolute assurance that when labor again caught up its pick the manager's word would command instant obedience.

The landlord, flushed with the exertion of their concoction, soon set the incomparable beverages before us. With the alacrity of a man who will have no shadow of debt hanging over his head, Don José thrust a hand into a pocket of his alpaca and cast on the table three mammoth coppers, the combined value of which was close upon five cents. With the first sip he rolled a cigarette and pushed pouch and papers toward me. Then having introduced me as

" Señor Newyorkano," he plunged headlong into the story of my life, addressing not merely the assembled miners but whomever else may have been prowling within gunshot of the building. " And to think, amigos," he concluded, " after crossing all the sea el señor should have wandered into San Pablo looking for a posada!"

The company beat their hands on the tables and howled with merriment. Whatever the uproarious humor of that climax to my adventures, it lost nothing of its poignancy as long as the evening lasted, and served to top off a score of otherwise pointless tales.

My ignorance of the Andalusian game notwithstanding, I had soon taken a hand. The alcalde, consuming uncounted cigarettes, beamed over my shoulder shouting praise of my sagacity each time I cast on the table the card he pointed out. As for " ponche," what the peerless libation lacked in favor with the masses it gained in the unswerving fidelity of its sponsor. With clock-like regularity his reverberating voice rang out above the din of revelry: " Don Gregario, un ponche!" In vain did I announce my thirst permanently abated, in vain did I " say the word " or strive at least to take advantage of the free choice offered me. My protest was invariably drowned in the roar of the amended order: " Sí, sí! Dos ponches, Don Gregario!"

Evening rolled into night, night into morning, and

still the clank of copper coins continued. Once I attempted to forestall the diving into that fathomless alpaca by thrusting a hand into my own pocket. My unquenchable host started to his feet with a bellow that seemed to set the very walls vibrating:

"Strangers, señor, cannot spend money in San Pablo! We are a private town!"

The minute hand was nearing the completion of its third lap when a general uprising, subtly instigated by the landlord, swept the carousers into the coal-black night. "My house" was no such regal mansion as befitted an industrial sovereign, an alcalde, and a man of unlimited coppers rolled into one. It was different, to be sure, from the other bare stone dwellings of San Pablo, but only in the wild bachelor disorder that reigned within its four naked walls. In one corner was a mountainous husk mattress. Its mate, alleged my host, lay somewhere buried in the jumble; and he verified the assertion not long after by dragging it forth. While he was booting this into some resemblance to a bed, I kicked off my shoes and sank into profound slumber.

Don José, too, awoke at sunrise. His generosity, however, was but a shadow of its former self. On the descent from the town he listened to my objections to the proposed charity without once proffering a reply. In the depth of the valley he halted and stared gloomily up at the steep, sun-glazed path to the station observing that Providence after all is the appointed guardian of the foolhardy. I thrust out a hand. He shook it dejectedly and, bidding me go with God and remember there is no drink equal to ponche, set out to clamber his way back to the village.

Beyond the curve that swept San Pablo into the past a stream brawled down out of the hills. I climbed a little way up the gorge and came upon a tumbled boulder that had stored up a pool of just the depth for a morning plunge. Further on the railway grew more winding with every mile. The hills increased to mountain spurs, and soon after came the mountains themselves, the parched and rock-tumbled Sierra de Ronda, fertile only with the memory of smugglers and intricate pathways. The route led through many long, sombrous tunnels, entrance into which from the blazing sunshine was like the diving into a mountain lake. Where the burrowings ended, the line became still more circuitous, leaping over abysmal, jagged gulleys by massive dry bridges.

I fasted all the day; for it was Sunday, and the few station buildings that appeared were deserted. Yet the privation passed almost unnoticed. Were a choice to be made I would willingly sacrifice any day's dinner for the unfailing sunshine of Spain, reinforced by the pleasure of knowing that with the new dawn another unclouded day will begin.

My night's halt was beneath swaying palm-trees.

A company of "guardias civiles"

A cork factory

Down through a ravine beside the track were scattered a few rambling houses, in one of which I found accommodations. Its owner was a peasant, battered with years, who sat before his dwelling smoking in the cool of evening with his three sons. One of these was a *guardia civil* who had seen all the provinces of Spain, and whose language in consequence was Spanish. His brothers, on the other hand, spoke the crabbed dialect of Andalusia. I caught the sense of most of their remarks only at the third or forth repetition, to their ever-increasing astonishment.

" Hermano," interrupted the guardia once, " you know you do not speak Spanish? "

The speaker fell silent and listened for some time open-mouthed to his brother in uniform.

" Caracoles! " he cried suddenly. " I speak no other tongue than you, brother, except for the fine words you have picked up at las Cortes! "

Which was exactly the difficulty. The " fine " words were of pure Castilian, for which the rural andaluz substitutes terms left behind by the Moor. Furthermore his speech is guttural, explosive, slovenly, more redolent of Arabic than of Spanish. He is particularly prone to slight the S. His version of " estes señores " is " ete senore." Which is comprehensible; but how shall the stranger guess that " cotóa e' l' jutí'a " is meant to convey the information that " la justicia es costosa? "

4

My evening meal consisted of a *gazpacho*, olives, eggs, cherries, blood-dripping pomegranates, a rich brown bread, and wine; my couch of a straw mattress in a corner of the great kitchen — and my reckoning was barely twelve cents.

Afoot with the dawn, I had soon entered the vast cork forest that covers all the northern slope of the sierra. Wherever a siding offered, stood long rows of open freight cars piled high with bales of the spongy bark; the morning " mixto " hobbled by bearing southward material seemingly sufficient to stop all the bottles in Christendom.

By rail Ronda was still a long day distant — but not afoot. Before the morning was old I came upon the beginning of the short-cut which my hosts of the night had described. It straggled uncertainly upward for a time across a rolling sandy country knobbed with tufts of withered grass and overspread with mammoth cork-trees, some still unbarked, some standing stark naked in the blistering sun. Then all at once, path, sand and vegetation ceased, and above me stretched to the very heavens the grilling face of a bare rock. I mounted zigzagging, as up the slate roof of some gigantic church, swathed in a heat that burned through the very soles of my shoes. A mile up, two guardias civiles emerged suddenly from a fissure, the sun glinting on their muskets and polished black three-cornered hats. Here, then, of all places, was to be my first meeting with these officious fellows, whose inquisitiveness was reported the chief drawback to a tramp in Spain. But they greeted me with truly Spanish politeness, even cordiality. Only casually, when we had chatted a bit, as is wont among travelers meeting on the road, did one of them suggest:

"You carry, no doubt, señor, your personal papers?"

I dived into my shirt — my knapsack, and drew out my passport. The officers admired it a moment side by side without making so bold as to touch it, thanked me for privilege, raised a forefinger to their hats, and stalked on down the broiling rock.

A full hour higher I brought up against a sheer precipice. Of the town that must be near there was still not a trace. For some time longer I marched along the foot of the cliff, swinging half round a circle and always mounting. Then all at once the impregnable wall gave way, a hundred white stone houses burst simultaneously on my sight, and I entered a city seething in the heat of noonday.

CHAPTER III

RONDA crouches on the bald summit of a rock so mighty that one can easily fancy it the broken base of some pillar that once upheld the sky. Nature seems here to have established division of labor. The gigantic rock bearing aloft the city sustains of itself not a sprig of vegetation. Below, so far below that Ronda dares even in summer to fling down unburied the mutilated carcasses from her bullring, spreads the encircling *vega*, producing liberally for the multitude above, but granting foothold scarcely to a peasant's hovel. Beyond and round about stretches the sierra, having for its task to shelter the city against prowling storms and to enrich the souls of her inhabitants with its rugged grandeur.

Travelers come to Ronda chiefly to gaze elsewhere. As an outlook upon the world she is well worth the coming; as a city she is almost monotonous, with her squat, white-washed houses sweltering in the omnivorous sunshine. Her only " sight " is the *Tajo*, the " gash " in the living rock like the mark of some powerful woodman's ax in the top of a tree-stump.

52

A stork-legged bridge spans it, linking two unequal sections of the town, which without this must be utter strangers. A stream trickles along its bottom, how deep down one recognizes only when he has noted how like toy buildings are the grist-mills that squat beside it pilfering their power.

Elsewhere within the town the eyes wander away to the enclosing mountains. The wonder is not that her inhabitants are dreamy-eyed; rather that they succeed at intervals in shaking off the spell of nature's setting to play their rôles in life's prosaic drama. As for myself, I rambled through her piping streets for half the afternoon because she is Spanish, and because my supply of currency was falling low. Ronda boasts no bank. Her chief dry-goods merchant, however — by what right my informant could not guess — boasts himself a banker. I found the amateur financier at home, which chanced to be distant the height of one short stairway from his place of business. When I had chatted an hour or two with his clerks, the good man himself appeared, rosy with the exertions of the siesta, and examined the ten-dollar check with many expressions of gratitude for the opportunity.

" We shall take pleasure," he said, " in liquidating this obligation. You will, of course, bring persons of my acquaintance to establish your identity, como es costumbre in large financial transactions? "

I had never so fully realized how convincing was

my command of Spanish as when I had succeeded within an hour in convincing this bond-slave of " costumbre " that express-checks are designed to avoid just this difficulty. He expressed a desire to examine the document more thoroughly and retired with it to the depths of his establishment. Toward evening he returned with pen and ink-horn.

" I accept the obligation," he announced, " and shall pay you fifty-seven pesetas, according to yesterday's quotation on the Borsa. But I find I have such a sum on hand only in coppers."

" Which would weigh," I murmured, after the necessary calculation, " something over thirty pounds. You will permit me, señor, to express my deep gratitude — and to worry along for the time being with the money in pocket."

Travelers who arraign Ronda for lack of creature comforts can never have been assigned the quarters a peseta won me for the night in the " Parador de Vista Hermosa." The room was a house in itself, peculiarly clean and home-like, and furnished not only with the necessities of bed, chairs, and taper-lighted effigy of the Virgin, but with table, wash-stand, and even a bar of soap, the first I had seen in the land except that in my own knapsack. When the sun had fallen powerless behind the sierra, I drew the green reed shade and found before my window a little *rejaed* balcony hanging so directly over the Tajo that the butt of a cigarette fell whirl-

A Moorish gate of Ronda

ing down, down to the very bottom of the gorge.
I dragged a chair out into the dusk and sat smoking
beneath the star-sprinkled sky long past a pedestrian's
bedtime, the unbroken music of the Guadalvin far
below ascending to mingle with the murmur of the
strolling city.

To the north of Ronda begins a highway that
goes down through a country as arid and rock-
strewn as the anti-Lebanon. Here, too, is much of
the Arab's contempt for roads. Donkeys bearing
singing men tripped by along hard-beaten paths just
far enough off the public way to be no part of it.
Now and again donkey and trail rambled away in-
dependently over the thirsty hills, perhaps to return
an hour beyond, more often to be swallowed up in
the unknown. The untraveled carretera lay inches
deep in fine white dust. Far and near the landscape
was touched only with a few slight patches of
viridity. The solitary tree under which I tossed
through an hour of siesta cast the stringy, wavering
shade of a bean-pole.

Sharp-eyed with appetite, I came near, nevertheless, to passing unseen early in the afternoon a village hidden in plain sight along the flank of a reddish, barren hill. In this, too, Andalusia resembles
Asia Minor; her hamlets are so often of the same
colored or colorless rocks as the hills on which they
are built as frequently to escape the eye. I forded
a bone-dry brook and climbed into the tumbled.

pueblo.   Toward the end of the principal lack of a
street one of the crumbling hovel-fronts was scrawled
in faded red, with the Spaniard's innocent indis-
tinction between the second and twenty-second letters
of the alphabet:

Aqui se bende bino

Once admitted to the sleepy interior, I regaled myself on bread, cheese, and " bino " and scrambled back
to the highway.   It wandered more and more errat-
ically, slinking often around hills that a bit of exertion would have surmounted.   I recalled the in-
dependence of the donkeys and, picking up a path at
an elbow of the route, struck off across the rugged
country.

But there is sound truth, as in all his venerable if
somewhat baggy-kneed proverbs, in the Spaniard's
assertion that " no hay atajo sin trabajo."   In this
short-cut there was work and to spare.   As long as
the day lasted the way continued stiff and stony,
ceaselessly mounting or descending, with never a
level of breathing-space breadth nor a moment's respite from the rampant sunshine.   A few times I
stumbled upon an inhabited heap of stones in a fold
of the hills.   Man, at least fully clothed, seemed
never before to have strayed thus far afield.   From
each hutch poured forth a shaggy fellow with his
draggled mate and a flock of half-naked children,

all to stare speechlessly after me as long as the crown of my hat remained in sight.

The highway had deserted me entirely. As darkness came on, the dimming outline of the cragged hills rising on either hand carried the thoughts more than ever back to the savage, Bedouin-skulking solitudes of Asia Minor. Long after these, too, had blended into the night I stumbled on. At length there fell on my ear the distant dismal howling of dogs. I pressed forward, and when the sound had grown to a discordant uproar plunged, stick in hand, into a chaos of buildings jumbled together on a rocky ridge,— the village of Peñarruria.

The twisting, shoulder-broad channels between the predelugian hovels were strewn with cobblestones, no two of equal size or height, but all polished icy smooth. I sprawled and skated among them, a prey to embarrassment for my clumsiness, until my confusion was suddenly dispelled by the pleasure of seeing a native fall down, a buxom girl of eighteen who suffered thus for her pride in putting on shoes. Throughout the town these were rare, and stockings more so.

The *venta* into which I straggled at last was the replica of an Arabic *khan*, as ancient as the days of Tarik. It consisted of a covered barnyard court surrounded by a vast corridor, with rock arches and pillars, beneath which mules, *borricos*, and a horse or two were munching. One archway near the entrance was given over to human occupation. The *posadero* grumbled at me a word of greeting; his wife snarled interminably over her pots and jars in preparing me a meager supper. Now and again as I ate, an *arriero* arrived and led his animal through the dining-room to the stable. I steeled myself to endure a rough and stony night.

When I had sipped the last of my wine, however, the hostess, sullen as ever, mounted three stone steps in the depth of the archway and lighted me into a room that was strikingly in contrast with the dungeon-like inn proper. The chamber was neatly, even daintily furnished, the walls decorated college-fashion with pictures of every size and variety, the tile floor carpeted with a thick rug, the bed veiled with lace curtains. It was distinctly a feminine room; and as I undressed the certainty grew upon me that I had dispossessed for the night the daughter of the house, who had turned out to be none other than that maid whose pride-shod downfall had so relieved my embarrassment. Evidently the venta of Peñarruria afforded no other accommodations befitting a guest who could squander more than a half peseta for a mere night's lodging.

Over the head of the bed, framed in flowers and the dust-dry memento of Palm Sunday, was a chromo misrepresentation of the Virgin, beneath which flickered a wick floating in oil. I was early trained to sleep in darkness. When I had endured for a

A fishman of Malaga

A Spanish highway

long half-hour the dancing of the light on my eyelids, I rose to blow it out, and sank quickly into
slumber.

I had all but finished my coffee and wedge of black
bread next morning when a double shriek announced
that my forgotten sacrilege had been discovered.
The modern vestal virgins, in the persons of the
posadera and her now barefoot daughter, charged
fire-eyed out of my erstwhile quarters and swooped
down upon me like two lineal descendants of the
Grecian Furies. I mustered such expression of in-
nocence and fearlessness as I was able and listened in
silence. They exhausted in time their stock of blistering adjectives and dashed together into the street
publishing their grievance to all Peñarruria. Gradually the shrill voices died away in the contorted
village, and with them my apprehension of figuring
in some modern auto da fé. As I was picking up
my knapsack, however, an urchin burst in upon me
shouting that the guardia civil thereby summoned me
into his presence.

" Ha," thought I, " Spain has merely grown more
up-to-date in dealing with heretics."

The officer was not to be avoided. He sat before
a building which I must pass to escape from the
town ; a deep-eyed man who manipulated his cigarette
with one hand while he slowly ran the fingers of the
other through the only beard, perhaps, in all the
dreaded company of which he was a member. His

greeting, however, was cordial, almost diffident. In fact, the cause of my summons was quite other than I had apprehended. Having learned my nationality from the inn register, he had made so bold as to hope that I would delay my departure long enough to give him a cigarette's worth of information concerning the western hemisphere.

" I have resigned from the guardia," he said in explanation of his un-Spanish curiosity, " and in three months I go to make cigars in your Tampa, in la Florida. Spain can no longer feed her children."

I sketched briefly the life in the new world, not forgetting to picture some of the hardships such a change must bring a man of the fixed habits of forty, and took leave of him with the national benediction.

For some hours I trudged on across a country similar to that of the day before. The heat was African. The Spanish summer resembles an intermittent fever; with nightfall comes an inner assurance that the worst is over, and infallibly with the new day the blazing sun sends down its rays seemingly more fiercely than before. The reflection of how agreeable would be a respite from its fury was weaving itself into my thoughts when I swooped suddenly down upon a railway at a hamlet named Gobantes. I had no hope of covering all Spain afoot. Away among the hills to the north the

whistle of a locomotive that moment sounded. I
turned aside to the station and bought a ticket to
Málaga.

The train squirmed away through howling, arid
mountains, abounding in tunnels and tumbled bottomless gorges; then descending headlong to the
plain, landed me at the seaport in mid-afternoon.
Even Málaga on the seashore suffers from the heat.
Her Alameda was thick in dust as an Andalusian
highway; beneath the choking trees that bordered
it the stone benches were blistering to the touch.
The excursion was rewarded, however, if by nothing
more than the mighty view of the sail-flecked
Mediterranean from the summit of the Gibilfaro,
reached by a dripping climb through shifting rubble
and swarms of begging gypsy children. Africa
was visible, dimly but unmistakably. Below sim-
mered the city, unenlivened by a single touch of
green; to the right the vega stretched floor-level to
the foot of the treeless Alhama. Directly beneath
me, like some vast tub, yawned the bullring, empty
now but for a score of boys playing at " torero,"
flaunting their jackets in the face of an urchin fitted
with paper horns, and dashing in pretended terror
for the barrier when he turned upon them. The
ascent of the Gibilfaro must certainly be forbidden
on Sunday afternoons. From this height the struggle in the arena, visible in its entirety, yet purged
by distance of its unpleasing details, would be a

scene more impressive than from the best seat in the tribunes.

When I reached the station next morning the platform gate was locked and the train I had hoped to take was legally departed. A railway hanger-on, in rags and hemp sandals, however, climbed the iron picket fence and shouted a word to the engineer. Then beckoning to me to follow, he trotted back into the building and rapped authoritatively on the closed window of the ticket-office.

"Señor," he said, as the agent looked out upon us, "be kind enough to sell this caballero a ticket."

"The train is gone," answered the agent.

"Not so, señor," replied the bundle of rags haughtily; "I am having it held that this cavalier may take it."

"Ah, very well," responded the official; and having sold me the ticket, he handed to the hanger-on the key to the platform gate. As I passed through it the latter held out his hand, into which I dropped a copper.

"Muchísimas gracias, caballero," he said, bowing profoundly, "and may your grace forever travel with God."

It was noon when I descended at Bobadilla, the sand-swept junction where all southern Spain changes cars. The train to Granada was soon jolting away to the eastward. Within the third-class compartment the heat was flesh-smelting. The bare

wooden cell, of the size of a piano-crate, was packed
not merely to its lawful and unreasonable capacity
of ten persons, but with all the personal chattels
under which nine of those persons had been able to
totter down to the station.   Between the two plank
benches, that danced up and down so like the screen
of a threshing machine as to deceive the blind man
beside me into the ludicrous notion that the train
was moving rapidly, was heaped a cart-load.   To
attempt an inventory thereof would be to name everything bulky, unpleasing, and sharp-cornered that
ever falls into the possession of the Spanish peasant.
Suffice it to specify that at the summit of the heap
swayed a crate of chickens whose cackling sounded
without hint of interruption from Bobadilla to the
end of the journey.

The national characteristics of third-class are
clearly marked.   Before a French train is well under
way two men are sure to fall into some heated dispute,
to which their companions give undivided but speech-
less attention.   The German rides in moody silence;
the Italian babbles incessantly of nothing.   An Englishman endures a third-class journey frozen-fea-
tured as if he were striving to convince his fellows
that he has been thus reduced for once because he
has bestowed his purse on the worthy poor.   But the
truly democratic Spaniard settles down by the com-
partmentful into a cheery family.   Not one of
my fellow-sufferers but had some reminiscence to

relate, not a question arose to which each did not
offer his frank opinion.   He who descended carried
away with him the benediction of all; the newcomer
became in a twinkling a full-fledged member of the
impromptu brotherhood.

Nine times I was fervently entreated to partake of
a traveler's lunch, and my offer to share my own
afternoon nibble was as many times declined with
wishes for good appetite and digestion.   Travelers
who assure us that this custom inherited from the
Moor has died out in Spain are in error; it is dead
only among foreigners in first-class carriages and
tourist hotels — who never had it.   The genuine
Spaniard would sooner slap his neighbor in the face
than to eat before him without begging him to share
the repast.

We halted more than frequently.   On each such
occasion there sounded above the last screech of the
brakes the drone of a guard announcing the length
of the stay.   Little less often the traveler in the
further corner of the compartment squirmed his way
to the door and departed.   With a sigh of relief the
survivors divided the space equitably between them
— and were incontinently called upon to yield it up
again as some dust-cloaked peasant flung his bag of
implements against my legs with a cheery " buenas
tardes " and climbed in upon us.

Then came the task of again getting the train
under way.   The brusk " all aboard " of our own

land would be unbearably rude to the gentle Spanish
ear. Whence every station, large or small, holds in
captivity a man whose only duty in life seems to be
that of announcing the departure of trains. He is
invariably tattered, sun-bleached, and sandal-footed,
with the general appearance of one whom life has
used not unkindly but confounded roughly. How
each station succeeds in keeping its announcer in
the pink of dilapidation is a Spanish secret. But
there he is, without fail, and when the council of
officials has at length concluded that the train must
depart, he patters noiselessly along the edge of the
platform, chanting in a music weird, forlorn, purely
Arabic, a phrase so rhythmic that no printed words
can more than faintly suggest it:

"Seño-o-o-res viajeros al tre-e-e-en."

"Gentlemen travelers to the train" is all it means
in mere words; but rolling from the lips of one of
these forlorn captives it seems to carry with it all the
history of Spain, and sinks into the soul like a voice
from the abysmal past.

Among my fellow-passengers was the first Spanish priest with whom I came into conversational contact. In the retrospect that fact is all but effaced
by the memory that he was not merely the first but
the only Spaniard who ever declined my proffer of
a cigarette. To one eager to find the prevailing
estimation of the priesthood of Spain false or vastly
overdrawn, this first introduction to the gown

augured well. He was neither fat nor sensual; rather the contrary, with the lineaments of a man sincere in his work and beneficent in his habits. His manner was affable, without a hint of that patronizing air and pose of sanctity frequently to be observed among Protestant clergy, his attitude of equality toward the laity peculiarly reminiscent of the priests of Buddha.

At the station of San Francisco half the passengers descended. The building was perched on a shelf of rock that fell away behind it into a stony gulf. Surrounding all the station precinct ran a weather-warped and blackened fence, ten feet high, along the top of which screamed and jostled fully two score women and girls, offering for sale every species of ware from cucumbers to turkeys. Hucksters and beggars swarm down — or rather up — on San Francisco in such multitudes that the railway company was forced to build the fence for the protection of its patrons. But the women, not to be so easily outdone, carry each a ladder to surmount the difficulty. As the train swung on around a pinnacle of rock, we caught a long enduring view of the source of the uproar — the populous and pauperous city of Loja, lodged in a trough-like hillside across the valley.

Not far beyond there burst suddenly on the sight the snow-cowled Sierra Nevada, and almost at the same moment the train halted at Puente Pinos. I recalled the village as the spot where Columbus saw

The so-called " King of the Gipsies " — Granada

the ebbing tide of his fortunes checked by the messengers of " Ysabel la Católica "; but not so the priest.

" One of our great industries, señor," he said, pointing to several smoke-belching chimneys near at hand. " Puente Pinos produces the best sugar in Spain."

" The cane is harvested early? " I observed, gazing away across the flat fields.

" No, no," laughed the priest, " betabel (sugar beets)."

Spanish railways are as prone as those of Italy to repudiate the printed promise of their tickets. We descended toward sunset at a station named Granada only to find that the geographical Granada was still some miles distant. The priest had offered to direct me to an inn or I should perhaps have escaped entirely the experience of riding in a Spanish street-car. It crawled for an hour through an ocean of dust, anchoring every cable-length to take aboard some floundering pedestrian. Many of these were priests; and as they gathered one by one on either side of my companion, the hope I had entertained of discovering more of virtue beneath the Spanish *sotana* than the world grants oozed unrestrainably away. For they were, almost without exception, pot-bellied, self-satisfied, cynical, with obscenity and the evidences of unnatural vice as plainly legible on their countenances as the words on a printed page.

We reached at last the central plaza, where my guide pointed out a large modern building bearing across the front of its third story the inscription, " Gran Casa de Viajeros de la Viuda Robledo." As I alighted, a band of valets de place swept down upon me. I gave them no attention; which did not, of course, lessen the impertinence with which they danced about me. Having guessed my goal, one of them dashed before me up the stairs, shouting to the señora to be prepared to receive the guest he was bringing.

The widow Robledo was a serene-visaged woman in the early fifties; her house a species of family hotel never patronized by foreigners. We came quickly to terms, however; I was assigned a room overhanging the culinary regions, for which, with the customary two and a half meals a day, I engaged to pay four pesetas.

At the mention of money, the tout, who during all the transaction had not once withdrawn the light of his simian countenance, demanded a peseta for having found me a lodging. I reminded him of the real facts of the case and invited him to withdraw. He followed me instead into my new quarters, repeating his demands in a bullying voice, and for the only time in my Spanish experience I was compelled to resort to physical coercion. Unfortunate indeed is the tourist who must daily endure and misjudge the race from these pests, so exactly the antithesis of the courteous, uncovetous Spaniard of the working class.

I had not yet removed the outer stain of travel when a vast excitement descended upon Granada,— it began to rain. On every hand sounded the slamming of doors, the creaking of unused shutters; from below came up the jangling of pans and the agitated voices of servants. The shower lasted nearly ten minutes, and was chronicled at length next day in all the newspapers of Spain.

From the edge of Granada city a long green aisle between exotic elms leads easily upward to the domain of the Alhambra. In its deep-shaded groves, so near yet seeming so far removed from the stony face of thirsty Spain, reigns a dream-inviting stillness, a quiet enhanced rather than broken by the murmur of captive brooks. For this, too, remains in memory of the Moor, that the waters of the Genil and Darro are still brought to play through a score of little stone channels beneath the trees. There I drifted each morning, other plans notwithstanding, to idle away the day on the grassy headland before and below which spreads the vastness of the province of Granada, or distressing the guardians of the ancient palace with my untourist-like loiterings. But for her fame the traveler would surely pass the Alhambra by as a half-ruined nest of bats and beggars. Yet within she retains much of her voluptuous splendor, despite the desolating of time and her prostitution to a gaping-stock of tourists. Like so much of the Mussulman's building, the overshadowed palace is effeminate, seeming to speak aloud of that luxury and wantonness of the Moor in his decadent days before the iron-fisted reyes católicos came to thrust him forth from his last European kingdom. In this she resembles the Taj Mahal; yet the difference is great. For the effeminacy of the Alhambra is the unrobustness of woman, while the Taj, like the Oriental man, is effeminate outwardly, superficially, beneath all which shows sound masculinity.

In the city below is only enough to be seen to give contrast to the half-effaced traces of magnificence on the hill. He who comes to Granada trusting to read in her the last word of the degradation of the once regal and all powerful must continue his quest. Of squalor and beggars she is singularly free — for Spain. Something of both remains for him who will wander through the Albaicin, peering into its cave-dwellings, wherein, and at times before which romp brown gypsy children garbed in the costume in which the reputed ancestor of us all set forth from the valley of Eden, or occasional jade-eyed hoydens of the grotto sunning their blacker tresses and mumbling crones plying their *bachi* in conspicuous places. But even this seems rather a misery of parade than a reality, a theatrical lying-in-wait for the gullible *Busné* from foreign shores.

By night there is life and movement in Granada; a strolling to and fro along the Alameda to the strains of a military band, the droning of the water-

A Spanish railway station

carriers who bring down lump by lump the ice-fields of the Sierra Nevada, and a dancing away of the summer night to the clatter of the castanet. But by day — once only during my stay was the languid pulse of the city stirred during the sunlit hours. A conscript regiment thundered in upon us, blocking all traffic and filling the air with a fog of dust that dispelled for a time my eagerness to seek again the open road; a dust that thick-shrouded beneath its drab the very color of caisson and uniform, dry-blanketing the panting horses, and streaking the faces of men and officers with figures like unto the ornamental writing on the inner walls of the Alhambra.

CHAPTER IV

THE BANKS OF THE GUADALQUIVIR

GRANADA was sleeping a fitful Sunday siesta when I repacked my knapsack in the Casa Robledo. In the streets were only the fruit-sellers from the surrounding country, still faintly chanting over the half-empty baskets on the backs of their lolling asses. I paused to spend two " perros gordos " for as many pounds of cherries — for he who has once tasted the cherries of Granada has no second choice — and trudged away through the northern suburb leaving a trail of pits behind me.

The highway surmounted the last crest and swung down to the level of the plain. Like a sea of heat mist diked by the encircling mountains stretched the vega, looking across which one saw at a glance no fewer than a score of villages half concealed by an inundation of sunshine so physically visible that one observed with astonishment that the snow lay still unmelted on the peak of Mulhacen behind.

Yet for all the heat I would not have been elsewhere nor doing else than striking across the steaming vega of Granada. In such situations, I confess, I like my own company best. With the finest companion

72

in the world a ten-mile tramp through this heat and
dust would have been a labor like the digging of a
ditch.   Alone, with the imagination free to take color
from the landscape, each petty inconvenience seemed
but to put me the more in touch with the real Spain.

Just here lies the advantage of traveling in this
half-tramp fashion.   The "personally conducted"
traveler, too, sees the Alhambra; yet how slight is
that compared with sharing the actual life of the
Spanish people, which the tourist catches if at all in
vagrant, posing fragments?   To move through a
foreign country shut up in a moving room, carrying
with one the modern luxuries of home, is not travel;
we call it so by courtesy and for lack of an exact
term.   "Il faut payer de sa personne."   He who
will gather the real honey of travel must be on the
scene, a "super" at least on the stage itself, not gos-
siping with his fellows in a box.

With all its aridity the vega was richly productive.
Olive-trees hung heavy, on either hand spread
broad fields of grain in which peasants were toiling
swelteringly as if they had never heard of the common sense institution of Sunday.   When sun and
tree-tops met, the highway began to wind, leaving
the vega behind and wandering through low hills
among which appeared no villages, only an occasional
rough-hewn house by the way.   Toward twilight
there opened a more verdant valley, and a stream,
rising somewhere near at hand, fell in with the car-

retera and capered prattling along with it into the night.

It was ten perhaps when I came upon a lonely little venta by the wayside, a one-story building older than the modern world, serving both for dwelling and stable. The master of the house and her husband were both of that light-hearted gentry to whom life means nothing more than to be permitted good health and a place to eat an occasional *puchero*. With these and a pair of mountain arrieros I gossiped until my eyelids grew heavy, and turned in on a husk mattress spread, like that of my hosts, on the kitchen floor.

At the first hint of dawn I was off and had set the sun a handicap of three miles or more before he began to ruddy the jagged chain to the eastward. The family was already at work, the arrieros wending on their southward way singing savage fragments of song; for like the Arab the rural andaluz sleeps full-dressed and springs instantly from bed to labor.

A country lightly populated continued. At high noon I reached a bath-inviting irrigating stream that wound through a grove of willows offering protection enough from the sun for a brief siesta. Soon after, the landscape grew savage and untenanted, and the carretera more and more constricted until it passed, like a thread through the eye of a needle, through a short tunnel, built, said the inscription, by Isabel II — an example of exaggerated Spanish courtesy

A gitana of Granada

In the district of the Alhambra

evidently, for history shouts assurance that the activities of that lady were rather exclusively confined to less enduring works.   Once released, the gorge expanded to a rambling valley with many orchards of apricots and plums, still walled, however, by hills so lofty that the sun deserted it early and gave the unusual sight of a lingering twilight.

From sunset until well into the night I kept sharp lookout for a public hostelry; but only a few peasants' hovels appeared, and with fifty-six kilometers in my legs I gave up the search and made my bed of a bundle of straw on a little nose of meadow above the highway.   All through the night the tramp of asses and the cursing or singing of their drivers passing below drifted into my dreams.   The weather was not cold, yet in the most silent hour a chilliness half-arousing crept over me, and it was with a sense of relief that I awoke at last entirely and wandered on.

By daylight the hills receded somewhat, flattening themselves out to rolling uplands; the stream grew broad and noisy in its strength.   Then suddenly at the turning of an abrupt hill Jaen rose before me, a city pitched on a rocky summit like the capping over a haycock, in the center the vast cathedral; the whole radiant with the flush of morning and surrounded by a soil as red as if the blood of all the Moorish wars were gathered here and mixed with the clay.   The highway, catching sight of its goal, abandoned unceremoniously the guidance of the river and climbed with great strides up the red hillside into the town.

I had been so long up that the day seemed already far advanced. But Jaen was still half abed. I drifted into what was outwardly a little *cantina*, with zinc bar and shining spigots, but domestically the home of an amiable couple. The *cantinero*, lolling in the customary fat-man's attitude behind the bar, woke with a start from the first of that day's siestas when I requested breakfast, while his spouse ceased her sweeping to cry out, " Como! Tan temprano! Why, it is scarcely eight o'clock!" The lady, however, gave evidence of an un-Spanish adaptability by rising to the occasion. While Señor Corpulence was still shaking his head condolingly, she called to the driver of a passing flock of goats, one of which, under her watchful eye, yielded up a foaming cupful that tided me over until I sat down in the family dining-room to a breakfast such as is rarely forthcoming in Spain before high noon.

The cantina was no more a lodging-house than a restaurant. But so charming a couple was not to be lost sight of, and before the meal was ended I expressed a hope of making my home with them during my stay. The landlord was taking breath to express his regrets when the matron, after a moment of hesitation, admitted that even that might be possible, adding however, with an air of mystery, that she could not be certain until toward night. I left my bundle and sauntered out into the city.

Jaen is a town of the Arab, a steep town with those narrow, sun-dodging streets that to the utilitarian are inexcusable but to all others give evidence of the wisdom of the Moor. Content, perhaps, with its past history, it is to-day a slow, serenely peaceful place riding at anchor in the stream of time and singularly free from that dread disease of doing something always. Unusually full it seemed of ingenuous, unhurrying old men engaged only in watching life glide by under the blue sky. I spent half the day chatting with these in the thirsting, dust-blown park in the center of the town. Their language was still a dialect of Andalusia, a bit more Castilian perhaps than on the southern coast, at any rate now grown as familiar as my own.

Each conversation was punctuated with cigarette smoke. Nothing in Spain is more nearly incessant than the rolling and burning of what Borrow dubbed in the days before the French word had won a place in our language " paper cigars." We of America are inclined to look upon indulgence in this form of the weed as a failing of youth, undignified at least in old men. Not so the Spaniard. Whatever his age or station in life — the policeman on his beat, the engineer at his throttle, the boy at his father's heels, the priest in his gown, puff eternally at their *cigarillo*. The express-check cashed in a Spanish bank is swallowed up in a cloud of smoke as thick as the fog that hovers over the Grand Banks; the directors who should attempt to forbid smoking in their establishment would in all probability be invited to hump over their own ledgers. The Spaniard is strikingly the antithesis of the American in this, that his " pleasures," his addictions come first and his work second. Let the two conflict and his work must be postponed or left undone. In contrast to his ceaseless smoking the Spaniard never chews tobacco; his language has no word for that habit.

To the foreigner who smokes Spain is no Promised Land. The ready-made cigarettes are an abomination, the tobacco a stringy shag that grows endurable only with long enduring. Matches, like tobacco, are a fabrication — and a snare — of the government monopoly. Luckily, fire was long before matches were. These old men of Jaen one and all carried flint and steel and in lieu of tinder a coil of fibrous rope fitted with a nickled ring as extinguisher. Few peoples equal the Spaniard in eagerness and ability to " beat " the government.

I returned at evening to the wineshop to be greeted as a member of the household.

" You wondered," laughed the señora, " why I could not answer you this morning. It is because the spare room is rented to Don Luis, here, who works at night on the railroad. Meet Don Luis, who has

Ubiquitous features of Spanish church architecture

just risen and given permission that you sleep in his
bed, which I go now to spread with clean sheets."

The railway man was one of nature's satisfactions,
a short solid fellow of thirty-five, overflowing with
contagious cheerfulness. The libation incidental to
our introduction being drained, the landlord led the
way, chair in hand, to the bit of level flagging before
the shop. As we sat " al fresco " drinking into our
lungs the refreshing air of evening, we were joined
by a well-dressed man whom I recalled having seen
somewhere during the day. He was a lawyer, speaking a pure Castilian with scarcely a trace of the local
patois, in short, one whom the caste rules of any
other land of Europe would have forbidden to spend
an evening in company with a tavern-keeper, a switch-
man, and a wandering unknown.

" How does it happen, señor," I asked, when our
acquaintance had advanced somewhat, " that I saw
you in the cathedral this morning? "

" The domain of women, priests and tourists? "
he laughed. " Because, señor, it is the one place in
town where I can get cool."

Truly the heat of a summer day in Jaen calls for
some such drastic measure, for it grows estival,
gigantic, weighing down alike on mind and body
until one feels imperative necessity of escaping from
it somehow, of running away from it somewhere; and
there is no surer refuge than the cavernous cathedral.

This as well as the fact that the edifice contains considerable that is artistic led me back to it the next morning. But this time it was in the turmoil of a personally conducted party. When I had taken refuge in a shaded seat across the way, the flock poured out upon the broad stone steps and, falling upon a beggar, checked their flight long enough to bestow upon him a shower of pity and copper coins.

The mendicant was blind and crippled, outwardly a personification of gratitude and humility, and attended by a gaunt-bellied urchin to whom might fittingly have been applied the Spanish appellation " child of misery." Long after the hubbub of the passing tourists had died away in the tortuous city his meekly cadenced voice drifted on after them:

" Benditos sean, caballeros. Que Dios se lo pagará mil veces al cielo!"

A curiosity to know whether such gentleness were genuine held me for a time in my place across the way. Silence had settled down. Only a shopkeeper wandering by to a day of drowsing passed now and then; within the great cathedral stillness reigned. The urchin ran after each passerby, wailing the familiar formula, only to be as often ordered off. At length he ascended the steps stealthily and, creeping within a few feet of his master, lay down and was instantly lost in sleep, a luxury he had evidently not tasted for a fortnight.

The beggar rocked to and fro on his worthless

stumps, now and again uttering as mournful a wail
as if his soul had lost not one but all save a scattered
half-dozen of its strings. Gradually the surrounding silence drew his attention. He thrust a hand behind one of his unhuman ears and listened intently.
Not a sound stirred. He groped with his left hand
along the stones, then with the right and, suddenly
touching the sleeping child, a tremor of rage shivered
through his misshapen carcass. Feeling with his
finger tips until he had located the boy's face, he
raised his fist, which was massive as that of a horse-
shoer, high above his head and brought it down three
times in quick succession. They were blows to have
shattered the panel of a door; but the boy uttered
only a little stifled whine and, springing to his feet,
took up again his task, now and then wiping away
with a sleeve the blood that dripped from his face
down along his tattered knees.

Before the sun had reached its full strength, I
struck off to explore the barren bluff that overlooks
Jaen on the south and east. Barely had I gained the
first crest, however, before the inexorable leaden heat
was again upon me, and the rest of the day was a
perspiring labor. Only the reflection that real travel
and sight-seeing is as truly work as any life's vocation lent starch to my wilted spirits.

At intervals of two or three hundred yards along
the precipitous cliff that half circles the city stood
the shelter of an octroi guard, built of anything that

6

might deflect a ray of sunlight.   In the shade of each crouched a ragged, ennui-eyed man staring away into the limitless expanse of sunshine.   Their fellows may be found forming a circle around every city in the kingdom of Spain, the whole body numbering many thousands.   The impracticable, the quixotic character of official Spain stands forth nowhere more clearly than in this custom of sentencing an army of her sons to camp in sloth about her cities on the bare chance of intercepting ten-cent's worth of smuggling, when the same band working even moderately might produce tenfold the octroi revenues of the land.

I halted with one of the tattered fellows, whose gladness for the unusual boon of companionship was tempered by a diffidence that was almost bashfulness, so rarely did he come in contact with his fellow-man. For a long hour we sat together in the shadow of the hut, our eyes drifting away over the gray-roofed, closely-packed city below.   When our conversation touched on the loneliness of his situation the guard grew vehement in bewailing its dreariness and desolation.   But when I hinted that the octroi might perhaps be abolished to advantage, he sprang to his feet crying almost in terror:

"Por los clavos de Cristo, señor!   What then would become of nosotros?   I have no other trade whatever than to be guard to the octroi."

A sorry craft indeed, this squatting out a lifetime under a grass hut.

The bluish haze of a summer evening was gathering over Jaen when, returning through a winding street to my lodging, there fell on my ear the thrum of a solitary guitar and the rich and mellow voice of a street singer. The musician was a blind man of fifty, of burly build and a countenance brimming with good cheer and contentment, accompanied by a woman of the same age. As I joined the little knot of peasants and townsmen gathered about him, his song ended and he drew out a packet of hand bills.

"On this sheet, señores," he announced, holding one up, "are all the songs I have sung for you. And they are all yours for a perro gordo."

I was among the first to buy, glad to have paid many times this mere copper to be able to carry home even one of those languorous ballads so filled with the serene melancholy of the Moor and the fire of Andalusia. But the sheet bore nothing but printed words.

"Every word is there, señores," continued the minstrel, as if in response to my disappointment. "As for the music, anyone can remember that or make it up for himself."

To illustrate how simple this might be he threw a hand carelessly across his guitar and struck up another of the droning, luring melodies, that rose and fell and drifted away through the passages of the dimming city. Easy, indeed! One could as easily remember or make up for one's self the carol of the

meadow lark in spring or the lullaby of the nightin-
gale in the darkened tree-tops.

That I might catch the five-thirty train my host
awoke me next morning at three-twenty. I turned
over for a nap and descending in the dawn by the
dust-blanketed Alameda to the station two miles distant, found this already peopled with a gathering of
all the types of southern Spain. The train was due in
twenty minutes, wherefore the ticket-office, of course,
was already closed. After some search I discovered
the agent, in the person of a creature compared with
whom Caliban would have been a beauty, exchanging
stories with a company of fellow-bandits on the
crowded platform. He informed me in no pleasant
manner that it was too late to buy a ticket. When
I protested that the legal closing hour was but five
minutes before train time, he shrugged his shoulders
and squinted away down the track as if he fancied
the train was already in sight. I decoyed him into
the station at last, but even then he refused to sell
a ticket beyond Espeluy.

We reached that junction soon after and I set off
westward along the main line. The landscape was
rich and rolling, broad stretches of golden grain al-
ternating with close-shaven plains seething in the
sun. Giant cacti again bordered the way. Once, in
the forenoon, I came upon a refreshing forest, but
shadows were rare along the route. The line was
even more traveled than that below Ronda. Field-

laborers passed often, while sear-brown peasant women
on dwarf donkeys jogged by in almost continual procession on their way to or from market.

Not once during all my tramps on the railways
of Spain had a train passed of which the engineer
did not give me greeting. Sometimes it was merely
the short, crisp " Vaya! " more often the complete expression " Vaya V. con Dios! " not infrequently accompanied by a few words of good cheer. Here on
the main line I had occasion to test still further the
politeness of the man at the throttle. I had rolled a
cigarette only to find that I had burned my last
match. At that moment the Madrid-bound express
swung out of a shallow cutting in the hills ahead. I
caught the eye of the engineer and held up the cigarette in sign of distress. He saw and understood,
and with a kindly smile and a " Vaya! " as he passed,
dropped two matches at my very feet.

It was not far beyond that I caught my first
glimpse of the Guadalquivir. Shades of the Mis-
sissippi! The conquering Moor had the audacity to
name this sluggish, dull-brown stream the " Wad-al-
Gkebir," the " Great River! " Yet, after all, things
are great or small merely by comparison. To a people accustomed only to such trickles of water as had
thus far crossed my path in the peninsula no doubt
this over-grown brook, bursting suddenly on their
desert eyes, had seemed worthy the appellation.
But many streams wandering by behind the barn of

an American farmer and furnishing the old swim-
ming-hole are far greater than the Guadalquivir.

I crossed it toward three of the afternoon by an
ancient stone bridge of many arches that seemed
fitted to its work as a giant would be in embroider-
ing doilies. Beyond lay Andújar, a hard-baked,
crumbling town of long ago, swirling with sand;
famous through all Spain for its porous clay jars.
In every street sounded the soft slap of the potter; I
peeped into a score of cobble-paved courts where the
newly baked *jarras* were heaped high or were being wound with straw for shipment.

A long search failed to disclose a casa de comidas
in all the town. The open market overflowed with
fruit, however, stocked with which I strolled back
across the river to await the midnight train. It was
packed with all the tribes of Spain, in every sleeping
attitude. Not until we had passed Córdoba at the
break of day did I find space to sit down and drowse
for an hour before we rumbled into Seville.

I had exhibited my dust-swathed person in at
least half a dozen hotels and fled at announcement
of their charges, when I drifted into the narrow calle
Rosario and entered the " Fonda de las Quatro
Naciones." There ensued a scene which was often
to be repeated during the summer. The landlord
greeted me in the orange-scented patio, noted my
foreign accent, and jumped instantly to the conclusion, as Spaniards will, that I knew no Castilian, in

spite of the fact that I was even then addressing him
with unhesitating glibness. Motioning to me to be
seated, he raced away into the depths of the fonda
calling for " Pasquale." That youth soon appeared,
in tuxedo and dazzling expanse of shirt-front, extolling as he came the uncounted virtues of his house,
in a flowing, unblushing imitation of French.
Among those things that I had not come to Spain
to hear was Spanish mutilation of the Gaelic tongue.
For a long minute I gazed at the speaker with every
possible evidence of astonishment. Then turning to
the landlord I inquired in most solemn Castilian.

" Está loco, señor? Is he insane that he jabbers
such a jargon? "

" Cómo, señor! " gasped Pasquale in his own
tongue. " You are not then a Frenchman? "

" Frenchman, indeed! " I retorted. " Yo, señor,
soy americano."

" Señor! " cried the landlord, bowing profoundly,
" I ask your pardon on bended knee. In your Castilian was that which led me to believe it was not
your native tongue. Now, of course, I note that it
has merely the little pequeñísimos peculiarities that
make so charming the pronunciation of our people
across the ocean."

A half-hour later I was installed in a third-story
room looking down upon the quiet little calle Rosario,
and destined to be my home for a fortnight to come.
During all that time Pasquale served me at table

without once inflicting upon me a non-Spanish word. Nor did he once suspect what a hoax I had played on the " Four Nations " by announcing my nationality without prefixing the qualification " norte."

CHAPTER V

THE TORERO AT HOME

EVEN though one deny the right of its inhabitants to pity the man who must live and die elsewhere, even he who finds it panting and simmering in the heat of summer, will still count it no punishment to spend a fortnight in Seville. Tranquillity and that laggard humor so befitting vacation days reign within its precincts; yet it is a real city, never falling quite inert even at the hour of siesta, which is so like the silence of the grave in other towns of Andalusia. In the slender calle Rosario itself the stillness was never supreme, but tempered always by the droning of a passing *ajero* with his necklace of garlic, an itinerant baker, or a blind crone hobbling by with the fifth or the tenth of a lottery ticket, crooning in mournful voice, "La lotería! El numero trienta seis mil quinientos cincuenta y cinco-o-o. Who will win a fortune in the lotería-a-a?" Then above all else the soft, quarter-hourly booming of the cathedral bells to mark the passing of the day, like mile-stones on a wandering highway.

Nor with all her languor is Seville slovenly. Outwardly, like all that carries the ear-mark of the Moor,

she is bare. In the first brief survey one may fancy
one's self in a city of dismal hovels. But this is
because the houses are turned wrong-side out; a
glimpse into one of the marble-paved patios, fragrant
with orange-trees and cooled by fountains throwing their waters high in the dry air, forever dis-
pells the illusion.

My first full day in Seville fell on a holiday dedicated to San Pedro which, chancing also to be my
birthday, it was easy to imagine a personal festival.
In truth, the celebration of the day was marked by
nothing other than a bit more indolence than usual.
The real fiesta began at night in the Alameda of Hercules. There, among a hundred booths, the chief
object of interest was a negro, the first of his race,
one might fancy, who ever invaded the city.

By day, indeed, there is little else to do in Seville
than the royal occupation of doing nothing, a stroll
along the Sierpes in the morning, a retreat toward
noisy, glaring noonday to the cool and silent cathedral or those other churches that rival it as museums
of art, there to wander undisturbed among masterpieces of Spain's top-most century. The cathedral,
by the way, houses the most recent traveler in the
calendar of saints. Saint Anthony of Padua, not
many years ago, released by the dexterous knife of
an impulsive admirer, struck out into the unknown
and journeyed as far as our own New York. But
there repenting such conduct at his years or daring

to venture no further when his companion found a
sojourn in the Tombs imperative, he returned to his
place, and resumed it so exactly that only the sharpest eye can detect the evidence of his unseemly excursion.

A city that styles her most important street that
" of the Serpents," even though it harbors no more
of the outcasts of the pavement than many another
famous thoroughfare, may be expected to abound in
other strange names. Nor are they lacking. How
unworthy his lodging must the worldly Sevillian feel
who wanders uncertainly homeward in the small hours
to his abode in " Jesús del Gran Poder "—" Powerful
Jesus street." Or with what face can the merchant
turn off after a day of fleecing his fellow-man toward
his dwelling in " Amor de Dios "? Top-heavy
nomenclature is not confined to the streets. There
are many windows in which one may read the announcement of a " Media Noche de Jamón." No,
it is not a new law by the cortes, but a " Middle of
the Night of Ham," or, succinctly, the over-worked
ham sandwich. The uninstructed may be led at sight
of a building proclaiming itself an " Academia del
Tiro al Blanco " into the belief that Seville is overrun with institutions of higher learning. Not so,
distinctly not so. The " Academy of the Shot at
the White " is what less extravagant and imaginative
peoples dub a shooting gallery.

The man in the street is frequently no less colorful in his language. Yet the crisp, trenchant word common to that personage the world over is here, too, in full force, led by that never idle explosive "hombre." Dictionarically speaking, "hombre" means "man," and nothing more — which only proves how dismally the dictionary has failed to keep up with the times. For child, woman, or hen-pecked male answers to the expression as readily as to his own name. A sevillano leading a pup at the end of a string may be frequently observed to give a jerk at the leash and cry over his shoulder, "Hombre! Vámonos!"—"Come along, man!"

Anent the man in the street, it may be asserted that the Sevillian is usually there. Writers of Spanish romances have for centuries sought to win our sympathy for their love-lorn heroes by stationing them in the public way to whisper their pleadings through the cold bars of a reja. The picture is true; the lover of flesh and blood and of to-day still stands there. But so, for that matter, does the butcher's boy, the ol'-clothes man, and even less reputable persons. In Spanish newspapers the national wealth of phrase is too often overshadowed — like the news columns — by the touching assurance of personal announcements. Rare the page that is not half taken up with a black-bordered inset conveying the information that:

"Señor and Señora Pérez have the honor to advise their sorrowing friends and business associates that

little Willie Pérez, aged six, went up to heaven at
7:32 last evening."

There is nothing like being exact and punctual in
these little matters.

Toward sunset, after the siesta, it is not merely
à la mode but good sense to stroll down to the banks
of the Guadalquivir by the Golden Tower and drift
an hour or two back and forth along the deep-shaded
Alameda.   There one will be in the best company in
Seville — and the worst; for all the city is there,
lolling in its carriage or pattering along the gravel
in its hempen sandals.

But it is only at night that Seville is wholly and
genuinely awake and approaches somewhat to that
fountain of joy her inhabitants would have the world
believe her.   Then at last does she shake off entirely
the daytime lassitude.   The noises of the day are all
there, the street-hawkers have gained a hundredfold
in volume of lung, in number, and in activity, the
cathedral bells seem twice as loud.   Toward nine all
the city and his wife and children and domestics are
gathered or gathering in the great focal point, the
palm-fringed Plaza San Fernando.   The attractions
are several.   First of all is the " cinematágrafo," a
moving-picture machine throwing its mirth and
puerility on a sheet suspended in the center of the
plaza.   Second, a military band, not a caterwauling of strange noises that one would desire suppressed
by fire or earthquake, but a company seriously and

professionally engaged in producing genuine music, which it does from near nine till after midnight as continuously as any band could be expected to until some invention makes it possible to blow a trombone and smoke a cigarette at one and the same time. Third, there is the excitement which the mingling together in crowds brings every Latin people, and the supreme pleasure of strolling to and fro admiring one another and themselves. Fourth, if so many excuses are needed, there is fresh air and the nearest approach to coolness that the city affords.

Yet with all Seville gathered the thousand roped-off chairs around the curtain are rarely half filled; for to sit in one costs a "fat dog," as the Spaniard facetiously dubs his Lacedemonian two-cent piece. But what a multitude in the rest of the square! Out of doors all Spain mixes freely and heartily. Hidalgos with the right to conceal their premature baldness from Alfonso himself shudder not in the least at being jostled by beggars; nay, even exchange with them at times a few words of banter. Silly young fops, in misfit imitation of Parisian style, a near-Panama set coquettishly over one ear, trip by arm in arm, swinging their jaunty canes. Workingmen scorning such priggishness stride slowly by in trim garments set off by bright red *fajas* in which is stuck a great *navaja*, or clasp-knife of Albacete. Rich-bosomed *majas* with their black masses of mane-like hair, in crimson skirts or yellow

— as yellow as the gown of Buddha — drift languorously by with restless fan. No type is missing from the strolling multitude. Strolling, too, it is, in spite of the congestion; for the slow tide-like movement of the throng not only gives opportunity but compels any lazy foreigner to walk whether he will or not. Everyone is busy with gallantry and doing nothing — doing it only as the Spaniard can who, thanks to temperament, climate, and training knows that peerless art and follows it with pleasure, not with the air of one who prefers or pretends to prefer to be working.

The Sevillian is in many things, above all in his amusements, a full-grown child. Groups of portly business men, Seville's very captains of industry, sit hour by hour watching the unrolling of just such films as are shown in our " nickelodeons," shouting with glee and clapping each other on the shoulder when a man on the screen falls off a chair or a baker's boy deluges a passerby with flour. No less hilarious are the priests, shaking their fat sides with merriment at the pictured discomfiture of one of their guild in eager pursuit of some frail beauty. As interested as the rest are the policemen — and as little engaged in the fulfillment of their duties, whatever those may be. A poor species, a distressingly unattractive breed are these city policemen of Spain, in their uniform closely resembling checkerboard pajamas, lacking even the Hibernian dignity of size, stoop-shouldered and sunken-chested with lounging on their spines and the inordinate sucking of cigarette smoke into their lungs. Of the self-respect and pride of office characteristic of the national guardia civil they have none whatever. I recall no evening in the Plaza San Fernando that at least one pair of these wind-broken, emasculate caricatures of manhood did not fall to quarreling, dancing in rage and shrieking mutual curses in their smoke-ruined voices, while the throng dogged them on.

Families gather early in the plaza. There ensues a moment or two of idle thrumming — for father or brother is certain to bring his guitar — then out bursts the sharp, luring *fandango;* the little girls in snowy white squirm a moment on their seats, spring suddenly out upon the gravel, and fall to dancing to the click of their castanets as rhythmically as any professionals. They do not dance to "show off," they are indeed rarely conscious of attracting attention; they dance because the fire in them compels, because they wish to — and what the Andalusian wishes to do he does then and there, gloriously indifferent to whoever may be looking on. Let him who can imagine an American bringing his guitar to the public square of a large city and, surrounded by thousands, play serenely on into the depths of the night.

The Andalusian is one of the most truly musical beings on earth, in the sense that his music expresses

A Sevillian street

his real emotions. Song is almost his natural mode of expression, always spontaneous, with none of the stiffness of learned music. He has no prelude, follows no conscious rules, displays none of that preliminary affectation and patent evidence of technic that so frequently makes our northern music stilted and unenchanting. He plunges headlong into his song, anywhere, at any time, as a countryman unsullied by pedantry enters into conversation.

Thus wanes the night in the Plaza San Fernando, marked by the boom of the Giralda's bells, the bawling of vendors of lottery-tickets, of titbits, of matches, of *azucarillos,* of *naranjeros* crying their oranges, of boys carrying miniature roulette-wheels with a cone of sherbet as prize, that the little children may be taught to gamble early in life; and sharply above all else and most incessantly the alpargata-shod water-seller, with his vessel like a powder-can slung across one shoulder, his glasses clinking musically, crying, crying always in his voluptuous, slovenly dialect:

" A'ua! A'ua fresca! A'ua fresca como la nieve! Quién quiere beber? "

We have street calls in the United States, but he whose ear is daily assaulted therewith would have difficulty in imagining how musical these may be when filled, like the thrum of the guitar, the street ballad, the " carol of the lusty muleteer," and the wail of the railway announcer, with the inner soul of Andalusia.

7

There is to-day very little left of the national costume of Spain. One may except the stiff, square-cut sombrero, the alpargata of workman and beggar, the garb of the arriero, fitting and suiting him as if it had grown on him, the blanket which the peasant wears thrown over one shoulder, not because he realizes what a charm this adds to his appearance, but because he often sleeps out of doors or on the stone floor of public stables. Last, and least to be forgotten, is the mantilla. Except for it the women of Spain have succumbed to the ugly creations of Paris; may that day be centuries distant when the abomination masquerading under the name of woman's hat makes its way into the peninsula. Yet there is never among Spanish women that gaudy affectation of style so frequent elsewhere. Give her the merest strip of gay calico and the española will make it truly ornamental; with a red flower to wear over one temple and a mantilla draped across the back of her head she is more pleasingly adorned than the best that Paris can offer.

There is something unfailingly coquettish about the mantilla. It sets best, perhaps, with a touch of Arab blood; and in the Plaza San Fernando this is seldom lacking. Everywhere are morisco faces framed in the black mantilla and, as if in further reminder of Mohammedan days, there still remains the instinctive habit of holding a corner of the shawl across the chin. Thus accoutered only the Castilian

" ojear " can in any sense express the power given
the andaluza by her Oriental ancestry to do or say
so much with a glance of her black eye. With the
fan, too, she is an adept. The Japanese geisha is
in comparison a bungler. The woman of Spain has
her fan in such fine training that it will carry on
extended conversations for her without a word from
her lips, as Spanish peasants can talk from two hill-
tops miles apart by the mere motions of their arms.

But who of all the misinformers of humanity first
set afoot the rumor that the sevillana is beautiful?
" Salada " she is, brimming over with that " salt "
for which she is so justly renowned; chic, too, at
times, with her tiny feet and hands and graceful carriage; and always voluptuous. But one might wander
long in the music-livened Plaza San Fernando without espying a woman to whom could be granted the
unqualified adjective beautiful. On the other hand
it is rare that one meets a sevillana, unless she be
deeply marked by the finger of time, who is ugly;
never, if my search was thorough, one scrawny or
angular. In Spain is never that blending and mixture of all types as in our land of boundless migra-
tion; hence one may generalize. Salada, graceful,
full of languor, above all wholly free from pose, is
the sevillana in her mantilla. Of education in the
bookish sense she has little, of the striving after
" culture " to the divorce of common sense none
whatever. She may — and probably does — know

nothing of the sciences, or the wrinkle-browed joys of the afternoon club. But she is brimming with health and sound good sense, above all she is incontestably charming; and is not this after all — whisper it not in New England — the chief duty of her sex?

The Andalusian is primarily an out-door people; not merely in the plain and physical sense, but in life and character. He lives his life openly, frankly, setting his face in no mask of Puritanical pretension when he sallies forth into the world, being himself always, in public or in private. All in all among the sincerest, he is also the most abstemious and healthiest of peoples; not yet spoiled by luxury. His existence is reduced to simplicity; more exactly he has never lost touch with eternal nature. He takes time to live and never admits the philosophy that he must work before resting, but hinges his conduct on the creed that he must live first, and do whatever of work there is time left to do. In no sense is he lazy; rather in his sound sanity he has a real appreciation of the value of life. To-day is the great day to him. Live now is his motto, not put off living until he has earned enough to live, only to find it too late to begin. One would seek through Seville in vain for that strained, devil-chased air so stamped on our own national physiognomy. Whatever his vocation, or the hour of the day, the Spaniard has always time to choose the shady side of the street, time to halt and talk with his friends. As I watched him night by night in the Plaza San Fernando — and this is largely typical of all Spain — there came the reflection that the lands of continual striving, the lands where " culture " demands the repression of every natural emotion and enthusiasm, are dreary realms, indeed, compared with the living Latin South. Here is not merely animation, but life, real life everywhere, no mere feigned living.

On my second Sunday in Seville I attended my second bullfight. The first I had seen from the depths of the *sombra*, believing the assertion that none but a man with Arabic blood in his veins could endure the unshaded side of the arena. But my fear of sun-stroke had melted away; moreover, the sunside gate keeper is most easily satisfied. I bought a ticket at a corner of las Sierpes and entered the plaza as soon as the doors were opened.

Not a half-dozen had preceded me when I took a place on the stone bank directly behind the red *tablas*. On my heels appeared a rabble of ragged, joyful fellows, who quickly demonstrated that I had not, as I supposed, chosen the foremost seat, by coming to roost along the top of the barrier in front of me. One shudders to reflect what would befall individuals in an American baseball crowd who should conduct themselves as did these habitués of the Sevillian *sol*.

But to the mercurial andaluz, accustomed always and anywhere to give his idiosyncrasies and enthusiasms full play, the wildest antics seem quite in place.

If, as many reputed authorities will have us believe, the Spaniard's love for " toros " is dying out, what must it have been before the dissolution began? At any rate it has not yet sunk to that point where the vast plaza of Seville will hold all who would come, even to these *novilladas* in which the bulls are young and the fighters not yet more famous than a member of the cortes. From a dozen entries the spectators poured into the enclosure; in the blazing semicircle bronzed peasants and workmen with wine-swollen *botas,* across the shimmering sand richly attired señoritas in the white mantilla of festival, attended by middle-aged dueñas and, at respectful distance, by caballeros of effeminate deportment. The española is as ardent a lover of bulls as the men. One must not, however, jump to the conclusion that she is cruel and inhuman. On the contrary she is in many things exceedingly tender-hearted. Habit and the accustomed way of thinking make vast differences, and the fact that Spain was for seven hundred years in continual warfare may account for a certain callousness to physical suffering.

The Spanish plaza de toros is the nearest modern prototype of the Roman Coliseum; when it is filled one may easily form a mental picture of the scene at a gladiatorial combat. By four-thirty the voice

The Plaza, San Fernando

"A'ua! A'ua fresca! Quién quiere beber?"

of the circular multitude was like the rumble of some distant Niagara. Howling vendors of thirst-quenching fruits climbed over our blistering knees; between the barriers circulated hawkers of everything that may be sold to the festive-humored. Spain may be tardy in all else, but her bullfights begin sharply on time. At the first stroke of five from the Giralda a bugle sounded, the barrier gates swung open, and the game was on.

It would be not merely presumptuous, which is criminal, but trite, which is worse, to attempt at this late day to picture a scene that has been described a hundred times in every civilized tongue and in all the gamut of styles from Byronic verse to commercial-traveler's prose. But whereas every bullfight is the same in its general features, no two were ever alike in the unexpected incidents that make the sport of perennial interest to the *aficionados*. An "aficionado," be it noted in passing, is a "fan," a being quite like our own "rooter" except that, his infirmity being all but universal, he is not looked down upon with such pity by his fellow-countrymen.

Seville is the acknowledged headquarters of the taurine art. In our modern days of migratory mixture of races and carelessness of social lines, toreros have arisen from all classes and in all provinces — nay, even in foreign lands. One of Spain's famous *matadores* is a Parisian, and one even more renowned bears the nickname of the "Mexican Millionaire."

But the majority of bullfighters are still sons of
peasants and small landholders of Andalusia in general and the vicinity of Seville in particular. The
torero touring " the provinces " is as fond of announcing himself a sevillano as are our strolling
players of claiming " New Yawk " as home. Now-
adays, too, the bulls are bred in all parts of Spain
and by various classes of persons. But the *gana-
derías* of Andalusia still supply most of the animals
that die in the plazas of Spain, and command the
highest prices. Among the principal raisers is the
Duke of Veragua, who boasts himself — and can,
it is said, make good the boast — a lineal descendant
of that Christopher Columbus whose wandering ashes
now repose in the cathedral of Seville. The duke,
however, takes second place to one Eduardo Miúra,
whose bulls are so noted for their fury that a movement has for some time been on foot to demand
double fees for facing animals from his pastures.

The bulls of both my Sundays in Seville were
" miúras," and fully sustained the fame of their
ganadero. Each córrida began with the usual caparisoned parade, the throwing of the key, the flee-
ing of the over-cautious *alguaciles* amid the jeering
of the multitude. Is there another case in history
of a national sport conducted by the vested authorities of government? Perhaps so, in Nero's little
matinées in the toasting of Christians. But here the
rules of the game are altered and to some extent

framed by those authorities. Imagine the city fathers of, let us say Boston, debating with fiery zeal whether a batter should be allowed to run on the third strike! Then, too, the mayor or his representative is the umpire, safely so, however, for he is securely locked in his box high above the rabble and there is never a losing team to lie in wait for him beyond the club-house.

It is the all but universal custom, I note in skimming through the impressions of a half-hundred travelers in Spain, to decry bullfighting in the strongest terms. Nay, almost without exception, the chroniclers, who appear in most cases to be full-grown, able-bodied men, relate how a sickness nigh unto death came upon them at about the time the first bull was getting warmed up to his business which forced them to flee the scene forever. One must, of course, believe they are not posing before the gentle reader, but it comes at times with difficulty. To be sure, the game has little in common with croquet or dominoes; there are stages of it, particularly the disemboweling of helpless hacks, that give the newcomer more than one unpleasant quarter of an hour. Indeed, I am inclined to think that had I a dictator's power I should abolish bullfighting to-morrow, or next Monday at least; but so, for that matter, I should auto races and country billboards, Salome dancers and politicians, train-boys and ticket speculators. Unfortunately —

At any rate, I came out to this second córrida in Seville and left it with the hope of seeing several more. Certainly there is no other " sport " that can more quickly and fully efface from the mind of the spectator his personal cares and problems; and is not this, after all, the chief, if not the only raîson d'être of professional sport? There is an intensity in the moment of a matador standing with steeled eye and bared sword before a bull panting in tired anger, head lowered, a hush of expectancy in the vast audience, the *chulos* poised on tiptoe at a little distance, an equine corpse or two tumbled on the sand to give the scene reality, compared with which the third man, third strike in the ninth inning of a 0–0 contest is as exciting as a game of marbles. It is his hunger for such moments of frenetic attention that makes the Spaniard a lover of the córrida, not the sight of blood and the injuries to beast and man, which, in his intoxication at the game itself, he entirely loses sight of.

The newcomer will long remember his first bull — certainly if, as in my own case, the first bandarillero slips at the moment of thrusting his barbed darts and is booted like a soccer football half across the ring by the snorting animal. Still less shall I forget the chill that shot through me when, with the fifth bull at the height of his fury, a gaunt and awkward boy of fifteen sprang suddenly over the barriers and shook his ragged blouse a dozen times

Above all Seville bulks the cathedral and la Giralda

The Golden Tower on the Guadalquivir

in the animal's face. As many times he escaped a
goring by the closest margin. The toreros did not
for a moment lose their heads. Calmly and dexter-
ously they manœuvered until one of them drew the
bull off, when another caught the intruder by the
arm and marched him across the ring to the shade
of the mayor's box. There the youth, who had taken
this means of gaining an audience, lifted up a mournful voice and asked for food, asserting that he was
starving — a statement that seemed by no means im-
probable. The response was thumbs down. But he
gained his point, in a way, for he was given a fortnight in prison. Incidents of the sort had grown so
frequent of late in the plaza of Seville as to make
necessary a new law, promulgated in large letters on
that day's programme. Printed words, in all probability, meant nothing to this neglected son of Seville.

Such occurrences are not always due to the same
motive. The impulsive andaluz is frequently not
satisfied with being a mere spectator at the national
game. A score of times the tattered aficionados
about me pounced upon one of their fellows and
dragged him down just as he was on the point of
bounding into the ring. Indeed, as at any spectacle
the world over, the audience was as well worth attention as the performance itself. On the blistering
stone terraces of an Andalusian sol animation and
comedy are never lacking. In his excitement at a
clever thrust the Sevillian often sees fit to fall —

quite literally — on the neck of a total stranger; friends and foes alike embrace each other and dance about on the feet, shoulders, or heads of their uncomplaining neighbors. There is a striking similarity between the bantering of a famous torero by the aficionados and the " joshing " of a favorite pitcher in an American ball park, but the good day has yet to come when the recorder of a home-run will be showered in his circuit of the bleachers with hats and wine-skins, handfuls of copper coins, and tropical deluges of cigars. Nor does the most inexcusable fumble call forth such a storm of derision as descends upon a cowardly bull. The jibes have in them often more of wit than vulgarity, as when an aficionado rises in his place and solemnly offers the animal his seat in the shade. The height of all insults is to call him a cow. Through it all, the leather wine-bottles pass constantly from hand to hand. A dozen of these I had thrust upon me during the fight, and tasted good wine each time. The proceeding is so antiseptic as to warm the heart of the most raving germ-theorist, for the bota is fitted with a tiny spout out of which the drinker, holding the receptacle high above his head, lets the wine trickle down his throat. The skins so swollen when the córrida begins are limp and flaccid when it ends.

It seems the custom of travelers to charge that the apparent bravery of the bullfighter is mere pseudo-courage. Of all the detractors, however, not one

records having strolled even once across the arena
while the fight was on.   In truth, the torero's calling
is distinctly dangerous.   The meanest bull that enters
a Spanish ring, one for whom the spectators would
demand   " banderillas   de   fuego "— explosives,—
is a more fearful brute than the king of a Texas
ranch.   Their horns are long, spreading and needle-
pointed; the *empresa* that dared turn into the ring a
bull with the merest tip of a horn blunted or broken
would be jeered into oblivion.   Not a year passes
that scores of toreros are not sent to the hospital.

The Spanish espada is almost invariably " game "
to the last.   The sixth bull of this Sunday's tourna-
ment was, as often happens, the most ferocious.   He
killed six horses, wounded two *picadores*, tossed a
chulo as high as a one-story house and, at the first
pass of Vasquez, the matador, knocked him down and
gored him in the neck.   A coward, one fancies, would
have lost no time in withdrawing.   Vasquez, on the
contrary, crawled to his feet and swung half round
the circle that all might see he was unafraid, though
blood was streaming down his bespangled breast.
The alguaciles between the barriers commanded him
to retire, but it was to be noted that not one of them
showed the least hint of entering the ring to enforce
the order.   The diestro advanced upon the defiant
brute, unfurled his red muleta, poised his sword —
and swooned flat on the sand.   The bull walked
slowly to him, sniffed at his motionless form, and with

an expression almost human of disdain, turned and trotted away.

" Palmas al toro ! " bawled a boisterous fellow at my elbow, and the vast circle burst out in a thunder of hand-clapping and cries of " Bravo, toro ! " while the wounded espada still lay senseless in the center of the ring.

He was carried off by his *cuadrilla,* and the *sobresaliente,* which is to say the " jumper-over," or substitute, marched as boldly into the ring as if accidents were unknown. Once begun a córrida knows no intermission, even though a man is killed. The newcomer took steady aim and drove the three-foot sword to the very hilt between the heaving shoulders ; then nonchalantly turned his back and strolled away. The bull did not fall, but wabbled off into the shade to lean up against the tablas as if he had suddenly grown disillusioned and disgusted with life, and the spectators, no longer to be restrained, swarmed headlong into the arena. I pushed toward the animal with the rest and just as I paused a few feet from him he dropped suddenly dead, his blood-smeared horns rattling down along the barrier.

On rare occasions the matador, disobeying the unwritten law that the animal must be despatched by a thrust down through the body, places the point of his sword just behind the horns and with the slightest of thrusts kills the bull so suddenly that his fall sounds like the thump of a barrel dropped from a

height.   Then does the spectator, the unseasoned at
least, experience an indefinable depression as if this
striking of a great brute dead by a mere prick in the
back of the neck were a warning of how frail after
all is the hold of the most robust on life.

As we poured out of the plaza, I halted in
the long curving chamber beneath the tribunes.
Twenty-two horses, gaunt, mutilated things, lay
tumbled pellmell together in a vast heap.   Brawny
men in sleeveless shirts were pawing them over.
Whenever they brought to light a mane or tail they
slashed off the hair and stuffed it into sacks; when
they dragged forth a hoof the shoe was quickly added
to the heap of old iron in a corner.   The bulls were
treated with far more deference.   Each lay in his
own space, and the group gathered about him wore
the respectful mien of soldiers viewing the last remains of some formidable fallen enemy.   On my
heels arrived the jingling mules with the last victim.
Two butchers skinned, quartered, and loaded this into
a wagon from the central markets in exactly eleven
minutes, the vehicle rattled away, and the week's
córrida was over.

The Spanish torero is all but idolized by the rank
and file, being in this respect vastly above our professional ball players.   There is little society except
the purely bluestocking to which he has not the
entrée; wherever and whenever he appears he is sure
to be surrounded or followed by admiring crowds.

The famous, the Bombita family, for example, which has given four renowned matadores to the ring — and one to each of my Sevillian córridas — Machaquito of Córdoba, and a half-dozen others of highest rank are distinctly more popular and honored than the king. Nor is this popularity, however clouded by a bad thrust, transient or fleeting. Pepete, who departed this life with exceeding suddenness back in the sixties because a bull bounded after him over the tablas and nailed him to the inner barrier, is to this day almost a national hero.

Of course every red-blooded Spanish boy dreams of becoming a bullfighter and would not think of being unfamiliar with the features, history, peculiarities, and batting av — I mean number of *cogidas* or wounds of the principal fighters. Rare the boy who does not carry about his person a pack of portraits of matadores such as are given away with cigarettes. On the playground no other game at all rivals " torero " in popularity. There is something distinctly redolent of the baseball diamond in the dialogues one is sure to hear several times on the way home after a córrida. A boy whom fate or the despotism of the family woodpile has deprived of the joys of the afternoon, greets his inhuman father outside the gates with a shout of, " Hóla! Papá! Qué tal los toros? — How goes it with the bulls — what is the score? " To which father, anxious now to regain his popularity, answers jovially, " Bueno,

A bull-fight as it is not. Goya's impressionistic caricature

chiquillo! Tres cogidas y dos al hospital.— Fine,
son! Three wounded and two in the hospital."

Having thus trod the very boards of the last act of
" Carmen " and passed a splendid setting for the
third in my tramp through the Sierra de Ronda, I
decided to celebrate the otherwise unglorious Fourth
by visiting the scene of the third. The great
government Fábrica de Tabacos of Seville is one of
the most massive buildings in Spain, and furnishes
well-nigh half the cigarettes and cigars smoked in
Andalusia. I passed through the outer offices and
crossed the vast patio without interference. When I
attempted to enter the factory itself, however, an
official barred the way. I asked why permission was
denied and with a wink he answered:

" Sh! Hace calor. It is hot, and las cigarreras
are not dressed to receive visitors. Come in the
autumn and I shall make it a pleasure to show you
through the fábrica."

" But surely," I protested, " there are men among
the employees who have admittance to the workrooms
even in summer? "

" Claro, hombre! " he replied, with another wink.
" But that is one of the privileges of our trade."

I strolled out around the building. Back of it,
sure enough, was a cavalry barracks, and any one of
a score of young troopers sitting astride chairs in
the shade of the building might have passed for Don
José. Some of them were singing, too, in good

8

clear voices; though rather a sort of dreamy *malagüeño* than the vivacious music of Bizet. But, alas! With Don Josés and to spare, when the factory gates opened and the thousands of *cigarreras* so famed in song and impropriety poured forth, not one was there who could by any stretch of the imagination be cast for Carmencita. Sevillanas there were of every age, from three-foot childhood upward; disheveled gypsy girls from Triana across the river; fat, dumpy majas; hobbling old witches; slatterns with an infant tucked under one arm; crippled martyrs of modern invention; hollow-chested victims of tobacco fumes; painted *sinvergüenzas;* above all, hundreds of hale, honest women who looked as if they worked to help support their families and lived life seriously and not wantonly. But not a face or even a form that could have seduced any young recruit to betray his trust and ruin his career. Fiction, frequently, is more picturesque than fact — and far less pleasing in its morality.

CHAPTER VI

TO the man who will travel cheaply, interlarding his walking trips with such journeys by train as may be necessary to cover the peninsula in one summer, Spain offers the advantages of the " billete kilométrico." The kilometer ticket is sold in all classes and for almost any distance, and is valid on all but a few branch lines. One applies at a ticket agency, leaves a small photograph of one's self, and comes back a couple of days later to receive a sort of 16mo mileage-book containing legal information sufficient to furnish reading matter for spare moments for a week to come and adorned with the interesting likeness already noted.

I made such application during my second week in Seville, and received for my pains a book good for two thousand kilometers (1280 miles) of third-class travel during the ensuing three months. The cost thereof — besides the infelicity of sitting to a photographer in a sadly mosquito-bitten condition — covering transportation, government tax on the same, printing and the tax therefor, the photograph and

115

the tax for that privilege, and the government stamp attesting that the government was satisfied it could tax no more, footed up to seventy-five pesetas, or concisely, thirteen dollars and thirty cents.

But — if there is anything in official Spain that has not a "but" attached it should be preserved in a museum — but, I say, the kilometer-coupons are printed in fives rather than in ones, and however small the fraction of distance overlapping, it costs five kilometers of ticket. Moreover — there is usually also a "moreover" following the "but" clause in Spanish ordinances — moreover, there are hardly two cities in Spain the railway distance between which does not terminate in the figures one or six. It does not seem reasonable to believe that the railroads were surveyed round-about to accomplish this result; it must be, therefore, that in the hands of Spanish railway measurers the kilometer is susceptible to such shrinkage as may be needful. At any rate — and this is the thought I had hoped to lead up to — at any rate it was very often possible, by walking six or eleven or sixteen kilometers, to save ten or fifteen or twenty kilometers of ticket; and the game of thus outwitting the railway strategists was incomparably more diverting than either solitaire or one-hand poker.

Thus it was that, though I planned to reach Córdoba that evening, I left Seville during the morning of July 8 on foot. In my knapsack was a

Cordoba's deceptive entrance

Suburban life in Spain

day's supply of both food and drink, in the form
of three-cent's worth of those fresh figs that abound
in Spain — the one fruit that is certainly descended
directly from the Garden of Eden. For miles the
route led across a desert-dry land as flat as a western prairie, grilling in the blazing sunshine. At
rare intervals an olive-tree cast a dense black shadow.
There was no grass to be seen, but only an occasional tuft of bright red flowers smiling bravely
above the moistureless soil.

Long hours the retrospect of the city of toreros
remained, the overgrown cathedral bulking gigantic
above all else. All the day through cream-white
Carmona on her hilltop — a lofty island in a sea
turned sand — gleamed off to the southward, visible
almost in detail through the truly transparent air
of Andalusia. I did not go to Carmona, near as
she is to Seville; I never care to, for certainly she
cannot be half so bewitching in reality as she looks
on her sheer-faced rock across these burning plains of
sand. To the north, beyond the brown Guadalquivir, lay the distance-blue foothills of the Sierra
Morena, dying away in the northern horizon.

It was twenty-one o'clock by her station time-
piece when I descended at Córdoba from the train
I had boarded in the dusk at Tocina. A mile's
stroll brought me to the city itself, and a lodging.
Poor old Córdoba has fallen on parlous times.
Like those scions of nobility one runs across now

and then " on the road," it is well that she has her
papers to prove she was once what she claims to
have been.   Surely none would guess her to-day a
former imperial city of the Caliphs, the Bagdad
and Mecca of the West.   Her streets, or rather her
alleys, for she has no streets, are bordered for the
most part by veritable village hovels.   Most African
in aspect of all the cities of Spain, this once center
of Arabic civilization looks as if she had been overwhelmed so often that she has utterly lost heart and
given up, expending what little sporadic energy she
has left in constructing a tolerable Alameda to the
station, either that she may have always open an
avenue of escape, or to entice the unsuspecting
traveler into her misery.

To the imagination the Córdoba of to-day is
wholly a deception.   Yet she may rest assured that
she will not be entirely forgotten so long as her one
lion, the cathedral, or more properly her chief
mosque, remains.   For in spite of Christian desecra-
tion, in spite of the crippled old women who are
incessantly drawing water in its Patio of the Orange-
trees, despite even the flabby, cynical priests that
loaf in the shade of the same, smoking their cigarettes, and the beggars at its doors like running
sores on the landscape, the Mesdjid al-Dijâmi of
Córdoba does not, like many a far-heralded " sight,"
bring disappointment.   Once in the cool stillness of

its forest of pillars one may still drift back into the
gone centuries and rebuild and repeople in fancy the
sumptuous days of the Moor.

This reconstruction of the past was not uninter-
rupted, however, on the morning of my visit. For in
the church, that heavy-featured intruder within the
mosque like a toadstool that has sprung up through
some broken old Etruscan vase, mass was celebrating.
I crossed before the open door and glanced in.
Some thirty strapping, well-fed priests were lounging in the richly-carved choir stalls, chanting a
resonant wail that was of vast solace, no doubt, to
some unhappy soul writhing in purgatory. There
was not the shadow of a worshiper in the building.
Yet these able-bodied and ostensibly sane men
croaked on through their chants as serious-featured
as if all the congregation of Córdoba were following their every syllable with reverent awe.

They interfered not in the least with sight-seeing,
however, being, as I have said, in the church proper,
an edifice wholly distinct from the mosque and one
which none but a conscientious tourist or a fervent
Catholic would care to enter. There were, nevertheless, certain annoyances, in the persons of a half-
dozen blearing crones and as many ragged and officious urchins, who crowded about offering, nay,
thrusting upon me their services as guides.

In time I shook off all but one ugly fellow of

about fifteen, who hung irrepressibly on my heels.
Mass ended soon after, and the priests filed out into
the mosque chatting and rolling cigarettes, and wandered gradually away. One of them, however,
catching sight of me, advanced and clutching my
would-be guide by the slacker portions of his rai-
ment, sent him spinning toward the door.

" Es medio loco, eso," he said, stepping forward
with a shifty smile and nudging me with an elbow,
" a half-witted fellow who will trouble you no more.
With your permission I will show you all that is to
be seen, and it shall cost you nothing."

I accepted the offer, not because any guidance
was necessary, or even desirable, but glad of every
opportunity for closer acquaintance and observa-
tion of that most disparaged class of Spanish society.
To one to whom not only all creeds, but each of the
world's half-dozen real religions sum up to much the
same total, the general condemnation of the priesthood of Spain had hitherto seemed but another example of prejudice.

This member of the order was a man of forty,
stoop-shouldered, his tonsure merging into a frontal
baldness, with the face and manners of a man-about-
town and a frequenter of the Tenderloin. For three
sentences, perhaps, he conversed as any pleasant
man of the world might with a stranger. Then we
paused to view several paintings of the Virgin.
They were images deeply revered by all true Catho-

lics, yet this smirking fellow began suddenly to comment on them in a string of lascivious indecencies which even I, who have no reverence for them whatever, could not hear without being moved to protest. As we advanced, his sallies and anecdotes grew more and more obscene, his conduct more insinuating. When he fell to hinting that I should, in return for his kindness, bring forward a few tales of a similar vintage, I professed myself sated with sight-seeing and, leading the way out into the sunshine to the stone terrace overlooking the Guadalquivir, with scanty excuse left him.

A walk across the stately old bridge and around the century-crumbled city walls lightened my spirits. In the afternoon, cutting short my siesta, I ventured back to the cathedral. The hour was well chosen; not another human being was within its walls. Unattended I entered the famous third *mihrab* and satisfied myself that its marble floor is really worn trough-like by the knees of pious Mohammedans, centuries since departed for whatever was in store for them in the realm of *houris*. Free from the prattle of " guides," I climbed an improvised ladder into the second mihrab, which was undergoing repairs; and for a full two hours wandered undisturbed in the pillared solitude.

Night had fallen when I set out on foot from Córdoba. The heat was too intense to have permitted sleep until towards morning, had I remained.

Over the city behind, in the last glow of evening, there seemed to rise again the melancholy chant, ages dead, of the muezzin:

" Allah hû Allah! There is no God but God. Come to prayer. Allah ill Allah!"

The moon was absent, but the stars that looked down upon the steaming earth seemed more brilliant and myriad than ever before. In spite of them the darkness was profound. The Spaniard, however, is still too near akin to the Arab to be wandering in the open country at such an hour, and I heard not a sound but my own footsteps and the restless repose of the summer night until, in the first hour of the morning, I arrived at the solitary station of Arcoléa.

There I stretched out on a narrow platform bench, but was still gazing sleeplessly at the sky above when a "mixto" rolled in at two-thirty. The populous third-class compartment was open at the sides, and the movement of the train, together with the chill that comes at this hour even in Spain, made the temperature distinctly cold. That of itself would have been endurable. But close beside me, oppressively close in fact, sat a woman to the leeward of forty, of the general form of a sack of wheat, in her hand the omnipresent fan. Regularly at two-minute intervals she flung this open from force of habit, sent over me several icy draughts of air, and noting the time and place, heaved a vast

" ay de mi!" and dropped the fan shut again —
for exactly another two minutes.

I slept not at all and, descending as the night was
fading at the station of Espeluy, shouldered my
bundle and set off toward the sunrise. Three kilometers more and there lay before me the great open
highway to Madrid, three hundred and seven kilometers away. I struck into it boldly, for all my
drowsiness, reflecting that even the immortal Murillo
had tramped it before me.

The landscape lay desolate on either hand, almost
haggard in the glaring sunshine, offering a loneliness of view that seemed all at once to stamp with
reality those myriad tales of the land pirates of
Spain. Indeed, the race has not yet wholly died out.
Since my arrival the peninsula had been ringing with
the exploits of one Pernales, a bandit of the old
caliber, who had thus far outgeneraled even that
world-famous exterminator of brigands, the modern
guardia civil. His haunt was this very territory to
the left of me, and not a week had passed since a
band of travelers on this national carretera had seen
fit to contribute to his transient larder.

But his was an isolated case, a course that was
sure to be soon run. The necessity of making one's
will before undertaking a journey through Spain is
no longer imperative. In fact, few countries offer
more safety to the traveler; certainly not our own.
For the Spaniard is individually one of the most

honest men on the globe, notwithstanding that col-
lectively, officially he is among the most corrupt.
The old Oriental despotism has left its mark, deep
to this day; and the Spaniard of the masses asks
himself — and not without reason — why he should
show loyalty to a government that is little more than
two parties secretly bound by agreement alternately
to share the spoils. Hence the law-breaker is as of
yore not merely respected but encouraged. Pernales in his short career had become already a hero
and a pride of the Spanish people, a champion war-
ring single-handed against the common enemy.

Without pose or pretense I may say that I would
gladly have given two or three ten-dollar checks and
as many weeks of a busy life to have fallen into the
clutches of this modern Dick Turpin. His retreat
would certainly have been a place of interest. But
fortune did not favor, and I passed unmolested the
long, hot stretch to the stony hilltop village of
Bailen, a name almost better known to Frenchmen
than to Spaniards.

There, however, I was waylaid. I had finished a
lunch of all that the single grocery-store offered,
which chanced to be stone-hard cheese and water,
and was setting out again, when two civil guards
gruffly demanded my papers. This was the only
pair I was destined to meet whose manners were not
in the highest degree polished. The screaming heat
was, perhaps, to blame. I turned aside into the

A herd of fighting bulls

The peasants' noonday

shade of a building and handed them my passport, which they examined with the circumspection of a French gendarme. In general, however, it spoke well of my choice of garb that I was rarely halted by the guardia as a possible vagrant nor yet by the officers of the octroi as a possessor of dutiable articles.

It would seem the part of wisdom in tramping in southern countries to walk each day until toward noon and, withdrawing until the fury of the sun is abated, march on well into the night. But the plan is seldom feasible. In all this southern Spain especially there is scarcely a patch of grass large enough whereon to lay one's head, to say nothing of the body; and shade is rare indeed. On this day, after a sleepless night, a siesta seemed imperative. In mid-afternoon I came upon a culvert under the highway and lay down on the scanty, dust-dry leaves at its mouth, shaded to just below the arm-pits. But sleep had I none; for about me swarmed flies like vultures over a field of battle, and after fighting them for an hour that seemed a week, I acknowledged defeat and trudged drowsily on.

Soon began a few habitations and a country growing much wheat. In nothing more than in her methods of husbandry is Spain behind — or as the Spaniard himself would put it — different from the rest of the world. Her peasantry has not reached even the flail stage of development, not to mention the threshing machine. The grain is cut with sickles. As it arrives from the field it is spread head-down round and round a saucer-shaped plot of ground. Into this is introduced a team of mules hitched to a sled, which amble hour by hour around the enclosure, sometimes for days, the boy driver squatting on the cross-piece singing a never-ceasing Oriental drone of a few tones. From each such threshing-floor the chaff, sweeping in great clouds across the carretera, covered me from head to foot as I passed.

It was some distance beyond the town of Guarramán and at nightfall that I entered a village of a few houses like dug-out rocks tossed helter-skelter on either side of the way. The dejected little shop furnished me bread, wine, and dried fish and the information that another of the hovels passed for a posada. This was a single stone room, half floored with cobbles. The back, unfloored section housed several munching asses. The human portion was occupied by a stray arriero, the shuffling, crabbed old woman who kept the place, and by a hearty, frank-faced blind man in the early thirties, attended by a frolicsome boy of ten. It was furnished with exactly four cooking utensils, a tumbled bundle of burlap blankets in one corner, a smouldering cluster of fagots in another, and one stool besides that on which the blind man was seated.

This I took, reflecting that he who will see Spain must not expect luxury. The real Spaniard lives

roughly and shows himself only to those who are willing to rough it with him. As I sat down, the blind
man addressed me:

"Hot days these on the road, señor."

"Verdad es," I answered.

"You are a foreigner from the north," he remarked casually, as if to himself.

"Yes; but how do you know that?"

"Oh, a simple matter," he replied. "That you
are a foreigner, by your speech. That you are
from the north, because you only half pronounce the
letter R. You said 'burro' in speaking of our four-
legged companion there, whereas the word is 'bur-
r-r-ro.' You have walked many leagues."

"What tells you that?"

"Carajo! Nothing simpler. Your step is tired,
you sit down heavily, you brush your trousers and a
thick dust arises."

Blindness, I had hitherto fancied, was an advantage only during certain histrionic moments at the
opera, but here was a man who evidently made it a
positive blessing.

"Your are about twenty-five," he continued.

"Twenty-six. You will be good enough, perhaps,
to tell me how you guessed that."

"What could be easier? The tone of your voice;
the pace at which your words fall. It is strange that
you, a foreigner, should be such an amateur of
bulls."

"Caramba!" I gasped. "You certainly do not learn that from the tone of my voice!"

"Ah! We cannot tell all our secrets," he chuckled; "we who must make a living by them."

Then in the night that had settled down he fell to telling stories, not intentionally, one would have said, but unconsciously, fascinating tales as those of the "Arabian Nights," full of the color and the extravagance of the East, the twinkle of his cigarette gleaming forth from time to time and outlining the boy seated wide-eyed on the floor at his feet with his head against his master's knee. He was as truly a minstrel as any troubadour that wandered in the days of chivalry, a born story-teller all but unconscious of his gift. When after a long time he left off, we drifted again into conversation. He was wholly illiterate and in compensation more filled with true knowledge and wisdom than a houseful of schoolmen. His calling for five and twenty years had been just this of roaming about Spain telling his colorful stories.

"Were you born so?" I asked late in the evening.

"Even so, señor."

"A sad misfortune."

"You know best, señor," he answered, with a hearty laugh. "I have no notion how useful this feeling you call sight may be, but with those I have I live with what enjoyment is reasonable and find no need for another."

The crippled old crone, who seemed neither to have known any other life than this nor ever to have been attired in anything than the piece-meal rags that now covered her, dragged the heap of burlap from the corner and spread it in three sections on the stone floor. On one she threw herself down with many sighs and the creaking of rusty joints, the second fell to my lot, and the blind man and his boy curled up on the third. The arriero carried his own blanket and had long since fallen to snoring with his head on the saddle of his ass and his *alforjas* close beside him.

There is one Spanish sentence that expresses the most with the least breath, perhaps, of any single word on earth. It is " Madrugáis? " and means nothing less than " Is it your intention to get up early to-morrow morning? " In these wayside fondas it calls always for an affirmative answer, for the bedroom is certain to be turned into the living room and public hall and stable exit at the first glimmer of dawn.

I was on the road again by four-thirty. Three hours of plodding across a rising country brought me to La Carolina, a town as pleasing in comparison with its neighbors as its name. Its customs, however, were truly Spanish, even though many of the ancestors of its light-haired populace were Swiss, and my untimely quest for breakfast did nothing more than arouse vast astonishment in its half-dozen

9

cafés, wrecked and riotous places in charge of disheveled, heavy-eyed " skittles." In the open market I found fresh figs even cheaper than in Seville and, asking no better fare, turned back toward the highway.

I had passed through half the town when suddenly I heard in a side street a familiar voice, singing to the accompaniment of a guitar. I turned thither and found the blind singer I had first encountered in Jaen, just on the point of drawing out his bundle of handbills. While his wife canvassed the group of early risers, I accosted him with the information that I had bought one of his sheets in Jaen a month before.

" Ah! You too tramp la carretera? " he replied, turning upon me a glance so sharp that for the moment I forgot he could not see.

" Sí, señor. Do you not also sell the music of your songs? "

" How can music be put on paper? " he laughed. " It comes as you sing. Are you going far? "

" To Madrid."

" Vaya! " he cried, once more posing his guitar. " Well, there is much to be enjoyed on the road — when the sun is not too high. Vaya V. con Dios, young man."

Beyond Las Navas de Tolosa the face of the landscape changed, the carretera mounting ever higher through a soilless stretch of angular hills of dull-

Farming in old Castile

gray, slate-colored rock. Above Santa Elena these
broke up into deep gorges and mountain foothills,
an utterly unpeopled country as silent as the grave.
I halted to gaze across it, and all at once, reflecting
on the stillness as of desolation that hangs over all
rural Spain, there came upon me the recollection
that in all the land I had not once heard the note of
a wild bird.

In the utter quiet I reached a deep slit in the
flanking mountain, and even the stream that descended along its bottom was as noiseless as some
phantom river. It offered all the facilities for a
bath, however, and moreover under an overhanging
mass of rock that warded off the sun had watered
to un-Spanish greenness a patch of grass of a few
feet each way. There I spent half the afternoon in
slumber. The highway shortly after plunged headlong down into the very depths of the earth,
squirmed for a time in the abyss, then clambered
painfully upward between precipitous walls of
gloomy slate to a new level. When suddenly, unexpectedly, almost physically there rose before my eyes
the picture of the Knight of the Sorrowful Countenance, ambling past, close followed by thickset, hale-
cheeked Sancho on his ass. For I had traversed the
pass of Despeñaperros; languid Andalusia lay behind me, and ahead as far as the eye could reach
spread the yet twice more barren and rocky tableland of La Mancha.

CHAPTER VII

SPANISH ROADS AND ROADSTERS

IN the gloom of evening I espied on a dull, sterile hillside a vast rambling venta, as bare, slate-colored, and marked with time as the hills themselves. Here was exactly such a caravansary as that in which he of the Triste Figura had watched over his arms by night and won his Micomiconian knighthood. It consisted of an immense enclosure that was half farmyard, backed by a great stable of which a strip around two sides beneath the low vaulted roof had been marked off for the use of man; the whole dull, gloomy, cheerless, unrelieved by a touch of color. Within the building were scattered a score of mules, borricos and machos. Several tough-clothed muleteers, with what had been bright handkerchiefs wound about their brows, sauntered in the courtyard or sat eating with their great razor-edged navajas their lean suppers of brown bread and a knuckle of ham. Even the massive wooden pump in the yard among an array of ponderous carts and wagons was there to complete the picture. Indeed, this was none other than the Venta de Cardenas, reputed the very same in which Don Greaves passed his vigilant night, where Sancho was tossed in a blanket and Master Nicholas, the barber, bearded himself with a cow's tail.

The chance betrayal of my nationality aroused in the arrieros a suggestion of wonder and even an occasional question. But in general their interest was as meager as their knowledge of the world outside the national boundaries. Not once did they display the eagerness to learn that is so characteristic of the Italian. For the Spaniard considers it beneath his dignity as a caballero and a cristino viejo to show any marked curiosity, especially concerning a foreign land, which cannot but be vastly inferior to his own. Four centuries of national misfortune and shrinkage have by no means eradicated his firm conviction, implanted in his mind by Ferdinand and Isabel in the days of conquest, that he is the salt of the earth, superior in all things to the rest of the human race.

Spain is one of the most illiterate countries of the civilized world, yet also one of the best educated, unless education be merely that mass of undigested and commonly misapplied information absorbed within four walls. Few men have a more exact knowledge, a more solid footing on the everyday earth than the peasant, the laborer, the muleteer of Spain. One does not marvel merely at the fluent, powerful, entirely grammatical language of these unlettered fellows, but at the sound basic wisdom that stands forth in their every sentence.   If their illiteracy denies them the advantage of absorbing the festering rot of the yellow journal, in compensation they have a wealth of vocabulary and a forceful simplicity of diction that raises them many degrees above the corresponding class in more " advanced " lands.

It is of the " lower " classes that I am speaking, the common sense and backbone of Spain.   The so-called upper class is one of the most truly ignorant and uneducated on earth — though among its members, be it noted, is no illiteracy.   The maltreated Miguel was adamantinely right in choosing his hero from the higher orders; no Spaniard of the masses could be so far led astray from reason as to become a Quixote.

It is noticeable that the Spaniard of the laboring class has almost none of that subservience born in the blood in the rest of Europe.   Not only does each man consider himself the equal of any other; he takes and expects the world to take for granted that this is the case, and never feels called upon to demonstrate that equality to himself and the rest of the world by insolence and rowdyism.   Dissipation he knows not, except the dissipation of fresh air, sunshine, and a guitar.   Nowhere in Christian lands is drunkenness more rare.   Like the Arab the hardy lower-class Spaniard thrives robustly on a mean and scanty diet; he can sleep anywhere, at any time, and to the creature comforts is supremely indifferent. One can hardly believe this the country in which Alfonso X felt it necessary to enact stern laws against the serving of more than two dishes of meat at a meal or the wearing of " slashed " silks. Yet the Spain of to-day is not really a cheap country; it is merely that within its borders frugality is universal and held in honor rather than contempt.

When the evening grew advanced, my fellow guests lay down on the bare cobble-stones of the venta, making pillows of the furniture of their mules, and were soon sleeping peacefully and sonorously. For me, soft-skinned product of a more ladylike world, was spread a muleteer's thick blanket in the embrasure of a wooden-blinded window, and amid the munching of asses and the not unpleasant smell of a Spanish stable I, too, drifted into slumber.

From dawn until early afternoon I marched on across the rocky vastness of Spain, where fields have no boundary nor limit, a gnarled and osseous country and a true *despoblado*, as fruitless as that sterile neck of sand that binds Gibraltar to the continent. It is in these haggard, unpeopled plateaus of the interior that one begins to believe that the population of the peninsula is to-day barely one-third what it was in the prosperous years of Abd er-Rahman.

At length, across a valley that was like a lake of heat waves, appeared Santa Cruz, a hard, colorless town where I was forced to be content with the usual bread, cheese and wine, the former as ossified as the surrounding countryside. In the further outskirts of the place I found a potter at work in a large open hovel and halted to pass the most heated hour with him. In one end of the building was a great trough of clay in which a bare-foot boy was slowly treading up and down. Now and again he caught up a lump of the dough and deposited it on a board before the potter. This the latter took by the handful and, placing it on his wheel, whirled it quickly into a vessel of a shape not unlike a soup-bowl. I inquired what these sold for and with a sigh he replied:

"Three small dogs apiece, cocidos (cooked)"— pointing at the kiln —"y cuantos — how many break in the glazing! It is no joyful trade, señor."

Once he left his work to munch a crust and to offer me a cigarette and a drink from his leather bota, but soon drifted back to his task with the restless, harassed look of the piece-worker the world over. As I sat watching his agile fingers a bit drowsily, there came suddenly back to memory the almost forgotten days when I, too, had toiled thus in the gloomy, sweltering depths of a factory. Truer slavery there never was than that of the piece-worker under our modern division of labor. Stroll through a factory to find a man seated at a machine stamping strips of tin into canheads at two cents a hundred by a few simple turns of the wrist, and his task seems easy, almost a pastime in its simplicity. But go away for a year, travel through half the countries of the globe, go on a honeymoon to Venice and the Grecian isles, and then come back to find him sitting on the self-same stool, in the self-same attitude, stamping strips of tin into canheads at two cents a hundred by a few simple turns of the wrist.

Three blazing hours passed by, and I found myself entering a rolling land of vineyards, heralding wine-famous Valdepeñas. The vines were low shrubs not trained on sticks, the grapes touching the ground. A dip in an exotic stream reduced the grime and sweat of travel, and just beyond I came again upon the railway. A half-hour along it brought me face to face with the first foreign tramp I had met in Spain,— a light-haired, muscular youth in tattered, sun-brown garb, his hob-nailed shoes swung over one shoulder and around his feet thick bandages of burlap. He was a German certainly, perhaps a modern Benedict Moll whose story would have been equally interesting in its absurdity. But he passed me with the stare of a man absorbed in his personal affairs and accustomed to keep his own counsel, and stalked away southward along the scintillant railroad.

I halted for a drink at the stuccoed dwelling of a track-walker. In the grassless yard, under the only imitation of a tree in the neighborhood, slept a roadster. Now and again the chickens that scratched in vain the dry, lifeless earth about him, marched disconsolately across his prostrate form.

" Poor fellow," said the track-walker's wife at the well, " he has known misery, more even than the rest of us.   Vaya como duerme! "

I sat down in the streak of shade that was crawling eastward across him.   He wore a ten-day beard and the garb of a Spanish workman of the city, set off by a broad red faja around his waist.   In one bulging pocket of his coat appeared to be all his earthly possessions.

There was no evidence of overwhelming " miseria " in the cheery greeting with which he awoke, and as our ways coincided we continued in company.   He was a Sevillian named Jesús, bound northward in general and wherever else the gods might lead him.

" For a long time there has been no work in Seville for nosotros, the carpenters," he explained, though with no indication of grief.   " This half year I have been selling apricots and azucarillos in the bullring and on the Alameda.   But each day more of Seville comes to sell and less to buy.   I should have gone away long ago, but my comrade Gásparo would not leave his amiga.   Gásparo is a stone-polisher and had work.

" Then one day I am taken by the police for I know not what.   When after two weeks I come out, Gásparo is gone.   But he has come north and somewhere I shall run across him."

Jesús had just passed through a marvelous experience, which he proceeded to relate in all his Latin wealth of language — though not in the phraseology of a graduate roadster:

"Mira V., hombre! Two nights ago, when my feet are worn away with more than ten leguas of walking on the railroad, I come to Baeza. It is dark, and I wander along the track to find a soft bank to sleep. On the short railroad that is at each station there is waiting a train of merchandise. Suddenly a great idea comes to me. 'Sh! Jesús,' I whisper, 'what if you should hide yourself away somewhere on this train of merchandise? It would perhaps bring you to the next station.'

"With great quiet I climb a wagon and hide myself between bales of cork. Screech! Brrr! Rboom! The train is off, and all night I am riding — without a ticket. But at Vilches the man that goes with the train with a lantern comes by and it is my curse to be making some noise, moving to roll a cigarette. 'Ya te 'pia!' (I spy you!) he cries. Vaca que soy! So of course I must get down. But mira, hombre! There I have traveled more than twelve miles without paying a perrito!"

I had not the heart to disillusion him with a yarn or two from the land of the "hobo."

In the telling we had come within sight of Valdepeñas. It was a "valley of rocks" indeed, though a city of good size and considerable evidence of industry, abounding with great *bodegas*, or wine warehouses. As we trudged through the long straight street that had swallowed up the highway, we passed the *taller* of a marble-cutter.

"It is in a place like this that Gásparo works," sighed Jesús, wandering languidly in at the open door. I was strolling slowly on when a whoop as of a man suddenly beset by a band of savages brought me running back into the establishment. Jesús was shaking wildly by both hands a stockily-built young fellow in shirt sleeves and white canvas apron, who was rivaling him in volubility of greeting. Gásparo was found.

Still shouting incoherently, the two left the shop and squatted in the shade along the outside wall.

"Hombre!" panted Jesús, when his excitement had somewhat died down. "I have told myself that by to-morrow we should be tramping the carretera together."

But Gásparo shook his head, sadly yet decisively.

"No, amigo. Jamás! Nunca! Never do I take to the road again. I have here a good job, the finest of patrons. No. I shall stay, and send for the amiga — or find another here."

With the dignity of a caballero, Jesús accepted the decree without protest, and wished his erstwhile comrade luck and prosperity. Then that they might part in full knowledge, he launched forth in the story of his journey from Seville. Gásparo listened absently, shaking his head sadly from time to time. When the episode of the amateur hoboing began, he sat up with renewed interest; before it was ended he was staring at the speaker with clenched fists, his eyes bulging, the cigarette between his lips stone-dead. From that great epic Jesús jumped without intermission to a hasty survey of the anticipated joys that lay between him and Madrid. Suddenly Gásparo sprang into the air with an explosive howl, landing on his feet.

" By the blood of your namesake! " he shouted. " How can a man stay always in one place? This daily drudgery will kill me! I will throw the job in the patron's face, and get my wages this very minute, amaguito, and we will go to Madrid together. Jesús María! Who knows but we can hide ourselves on another freight train! "— and crying over his shoulder some rendezvous, he disappeared within the establishment.

We sauntered on to the central plaza. It was utterly treeless and paved with cobble-stones; nor could we find a patch of grass or a shaded bench in all the neighborhood.

" Look here, señor! " cried Jesús, suddenly rushing toward a policeman who was loitering in the shade of a bodega. " Don't you have any parks or Alamedas in this val de peñas of yours? You call this a city! "

" Señor," replied the officer in the most apologetic of voices, " we are not a rich city, and the rain so seldom falls in La Mancha. I am very sorry," and touching a finger respectfully to his cap, he strolled slowly on.

Though the sun was low it was still wiltingly hot in the stony streets. Jesús, as I knew, was penniless. I suggested therefore that I would willingly pay the score of two for the privilege of retreating to the coolness of a wineshop.

"Bueno!" cried the Sevillian. "The wine of Valdepeñas is without equal, and of the cheapest — if you know where to buy. Vámonos, hombre!"

He led the way down the street and by some Castilian instinct into a tiny underground shop that was ostensibly given over to the sale of charcoal. The smudged old keeper motioned us to the short rickety bench on which he had been dreaming away the afternoon and, descending still lower by a dark hole in the floor, soon set before us a brown glazed pitcher holding a *quarto* — about a quart — of wine, for which I paid him approximately three and a half cents.

In all western Europe I have drunk the common table wine in whatever quantity it has pleased me, and suffered from it always the same effect as from so much clear water. It may be that the long tramp under a scorching sun and the distance from my last meal-place altered conditions. Certainly there was no need of the seller's assurance that this was genuine "valdepeñas" and that what had been sold us elsewhere as such was atrociously adulterated. Before the pitcher was half empty, I noted with wonder that

In the market district

I was taking an extraordinary interest in the old
man's phillipic against the government and its ex-
orbitant tax on wine.   Jesús, too, grew in animation,
and when the subterranean Demosthenes ended with a
thundering, " Sí, señores!   If it wasn't for the cursed
government you and I could drink just such wine as
this pure valdepeñas anywhere as if it was water!"
I was startled to hear us both applaud loud and long.
A scant four-cents' worth had seemed so parsimonious
a treat for two full-thirsted men that I had intended
to order in due time a second pitcherful.   But this
strange mirth seemed worthy of investigation.   I
sipped the last of my portion and made no movement
to suggest a replenishing.   A few minutes later the
old man had bade us go with the Almighty, and we
were strolling away arm in arm.

The sun was setting when we reached the plaza.
We sat down on the cathedral steps.   The Sevillian
had suddenly an unaccountable desire to sing.   He
struck up one of the Moorish-descended ballads of
his native city.   To my increasing astonishment I
found myself joining in.   Not only that, but for
the first and last time of my existence I caught the
real Andalusian rhythm.   An appreciative audience
of urchins gathered.   Then the sacristan stepped out
and politely invited us to choose some other stage.

Across the square was a casa de comidas.   We entered and ordered dinner.   The señora served us
about one-third of what the bill-of-fare promised,

and demanded full price — something that had never before happened in all my Spanish experience. I protested vociferously — another wholly unprecedented proceeding. The policeman who had apologized for the absence of parks sauntered in, and I laid the case before him. The señora restated it still more noisily. I declared I would not pay more than one peseta. The lady took oath that I would pay two. The policeman requested me to comply with her demand. I refused to the extent of commanding him to take his hand off the hilt of his sword. He apologized and suggested that we split the difference. This seemed reasonable. I paid it, and we left. Dark night had settled down. We marched aimlessly away into it. Somewhere Gásparo fell in with us. Somewhere else, on the edge of the city, we came upon a heap of bright clean straw on a threshing floor, and fell asleep.

CHAPTER VIII

ON THE ROAD IN LA MANCHA

IT was Sunday morning, the market day of Valdepeñas, when I returned alone to stock my knapsack. The plaza that had been so deserted and peaceful the evening before was packed from casa de comidas to cathedral steps with canvas booths in which the peasants of the encircling country were selling all the products of La Mancha, and among which circulated all the housewives of Valdepeñas, basket on arm. The women of the smaller cities of Spain cling stoutly to their local costumes, aping not in the least the world of fashion. These of Valdepeñas were strikingly different from the Andalusians, considering how slight the distance that separates them from that province. They were almost German in their slowness, with hardly a suggestion of " sal "; a solemn, bronze-tanned multitude who, parting their hair in the middle and combing it tight and smooth, much resembled Indian squaws.

From the northern edge of the city the highway ran straight as the flight of a crow to where it was lost in a flat, colorless horizon. The land was artificially irrigated. The first place I stopped for water was a field in which an old man was driving round and round a blind-folded burro hitched to a *noria*, a water-wheel that was an exact replica of the Egyptian *sakka*, even to its squawk, jars of Andújar being tied to the endless chain with leather thongs. The man, too, had that dreamy, listless air of the Egyptian *fellah*; had I had a kodak to turn upon him I should have expected him to run after me crying for " backsheesh."

Ahead stretched long vistas of low vineyards. The only buildings along the way were an occasional bare uniform stone dwelling of a *peon caminero*, or government road-tender. At one of these I halted to quench my thirst, and the occupant, smoking in Sabbath ease before it, instantly pronounced me a " norte americano." I showed my astonishment, for hardly once before in the peninsula had I been taken for other than a Frenchman, or a Spaniard from some distant province.

The peon's unusual perspicacity was soon explained; he had been a soldier in Cuba during the Spanish-American War. I readily led him into reminiscences. Throughout the war, he stated, he had fought like a hero, not because he was of that rare breed but because every member of the troop had been filled with the belief that once captured by " los yanquis " he would be hanged on the spot.

"And are you still of the opinion?" I asked.

"Qué barbaridad!" he laughed. "I was taken at Santiago and carried a prisoner to your country. What a people! A whole meal at breakfast! We lived as never before, or since.

"You were quite right, vosotros, to take the island. I do not blame you. It was competición, just competition, like two shop-keepers in the city. I am glad the miserable government lost their Cuba."

So often did I hear exactly this view from Spaniards of the laboring class that it may be considered typical of their attitude toward the late disagreement. The strange question has often been asked whether it is safe so soon after the war for a North American to travel alone in the interior of Spain. For answer we have only to ask ourselves whether a Spaniard traveling alone in the interior of the United States would be in any imminent danger of having his throat cut — even had we been defeated. In Spain there is vastly less, for not only is the Spaniard quicker to forgive and far less belligerent than he is commonly fancied, but there exists in the peninsula not one-tenth the rowdyism and hoodlum "patriotism" of our own country.

I stayed long and left with difficulty. Gregarious is man, and on Sunday, when all the world about him is at rest, even the pedestrian finds it hard to exert himself. A league beyond I came upon

the Sevillians lolling in the shadow of another isolated peon dwelling in what seemed once to have been
a village.

Jesús in his eleven-day beard hailed me from afar;
moreover, the Sunday languor was still upon me. I
stretched out with them in the shade of the building,
but the flies prevented us from sleeping. We crawled
into a peasant's cart under the shed — but the flies
quickly found us out. We crossed the road to the
ruin of a church, split almost exactly through the
middle of tower and all, and one side fallen. Within
it was a grassy corner where the sun never fell, and
even a bit of breeze fanned us. But the flies had
made this their Spanish headquarters. We decided
to go on.

In that only were we unanimous, for the Sevillians
wished to follow the railroad, a furlong away, and I
the carretera. I had all but won them over when a
freight train labored by.

" Ay! Ay! Los toros! " shouted the two in
chorus.

" Where? " I asked, seeing no such animals in
sight.

" En las jaulas, hombre! In the cages! " cried
Jesús, pointing to a flat-car on which, set close together, were six tightly-closed boxes each just large
enough to hold a bull.

" We go by the railroad! " shouted Gásparo, decisively. " Alma de Dios! Who knows but we may

One of Spain's great rivers — nearly knee-deep

be able to hide ourselves on a train that is carrying toros to the córrida!"

We separated, therefore, and struck northward, though we marched side by side within hailing distance until we were all three swallowed up in the city of Manzanares.

The bare-faced, truly Manchegan town was half-deserted, though the reason therefor was not hard to guess, for the bullring in the outskirts was howling as I passed. For all its size the place did not seem to boast an eating-house of any description. At last I halted before an old man seated in a shaded corner of the plaza, to inquire:

"Señor, what does a stranger in your town do when he would eat?"

"Vaya, señor!" he replied, with the placid deliberation of age, and pointing with his cane to the shops that bordered the square. "He buys a perrito of bread in the bakery there, dos perros of ham in the butchery beyond, fruit of the market-woman —"

"And eats it where?" I interrupted.

"Hijo de mi alma!" responded the patriarch with extreme slowness and almost a touch of sarcasm in his voice. "Here is the broad plaza, all but empty. In all that is there not room to sit down and eat?"

I continued my quest and entered two posadas. But for the only time during the summer the proprietors demanded my *cédula personal*. I explained

that Americans are not supplied with these government licenses to live, and showed instead my passport.
Both landlords protested that it was not in Spanish
and refused to admit me.   One might have fancied
one's self in Germany.   It was some time after dark
that I was directed to a private boarding-house that
almost rewarded my long search.   For the supper
set before me was equal to a five-course repast in the
Casa Robledo of Granada, and for the first time since
leaving Seville I slept in a bed, and not in my clothes.

In the morning an absolutely straight road lay
before me across a land treeless but for a few stunted
shrubs, a face of desolation and aridity and solitude
as of Asia Minor.   From the eastward swept a hot,
dry wind across the baked plains of La Mancha that
recalled all too forcibly the derivation of its name
from the Arabic *manxa* — a moistureless land.

At fifteen kilometers the highway swerved slightly
and lost from view for the first time the immense
cathedral of Manzanares behind.   On either hand,
miles visible in every direction, huddled stone towns
on bare hillsides and in rocky vales, each inconspic-
uous but for its vast overtowering church.   " Si la
demeure des hommes est pauvre, celle de Dieu est
riche," charges colorful Gautier; which, if the church
of Spain is truly the " demeure de Dieu," is sternly
true.   City, town, village, hamlet, a church always
bulks vast above it like a hen among her chicks —
rather like some violent overpowering tyrant with a

club. To the right of the turn one might, but for
a slight rise of ground, have espied a bare twelve
kilometers away immortal Argamasilla itself.

During the day there developed a hole in my shoe,
through a sole of those very " custom-made " oxfords warranted by all the eloquent Broadway sales-
man held sacred — whatever that may have been
— to endure at least six months of the hardest possible wear. Sand and pebbles drifted in, as sand
and pebbles will the world over under such circumstances, and for some days to come walking was not
of the smoothest.

Almost exactly at noonday I caught sight of the
first windmills of La Mancha, three of them slowly
toiling together on a curving hillside, too distinctly
visible at this hour to be mistaken by the most ro-
mance-mad for giants. The few peasants I fell in
with now and then were a more placid, somber people
than the Andaluz and, as is commonly the case in
villages reached by no railway, more courteous to
the roadster than their fellows more directly in touch
with the wide world.

It was that hour when the sun halts lingering
above the edge of the earth, as if loath to leave it,
that I entered the noiseless little hamlet of Puerto
Lápiche. It contained no public hostelry, but the
woman who kept its single shop cooked me a supper,
chiefly of fried eggs, which I ate sitting on a stool
before the building. The fried eggs of Spain!

Wherein their preparation differs from that in other lands I know not, but he who has never eaten them after a long day's tramp cannot guess to what Epicurean heights fried eggs may rise. How, knowing of them, could Sancho have named cow-heel for his choice?

The evening was of that soft and gentle texture that invites openly to a night out-of-doors. On the edge of the open country beyond, too, was a threshing-floor heaped with new straw that would certainly have been my choice, had not the village guardia been watching my every movement from across the way. When I had returned the porcelain frying-pan to its owner, I strolled boldly across to the officer and inquired for a lodging.

"With regret, señor," he replied, raising his hat and offering me the stool on which he had been seated, "I am forced to say that we are a small village so rarely honored by the presence of travelers that we have no public house. But —" he hesitated a moment, then went on "— the weather is fine, señor; the night is warm, the pure air hurts no one; why do you not make your bed on the soft, clean straw of the threshing-floor yonder?"

"Caballero," I responded, with my most Spanish salute, "a thousand thanks — and may your grace remain with God."

For the first time during my journey the heat was tempered next morning, though by no means routed,

by a slightly overcast sky. The wind continued.
The highway led on through a seared brown country,
for the most part a silent, smokeless, unpeopled land.
The windmills of La Mancha were numerous now
on either hand as the road sank slowly down to a gap
in the low, gaunt mountains of Ciudad Real. At
last it reached them and, picking its way through
the narrow pass of Lápiche, strode off again across
a still hotter, drier region, unmitigated even by the
wind, which had stopped short at the mountain barrier — a land flowing not even with ditch-water. I
halted but briefly at the large village of Madridejos,
peopled by a slow, dreamy-eyed, yet toil-calloused
peasantry, as if their world of fancy and the hard
stony life of reality never quite joined hands.

Hot, thirsty and hungry, I came in mid-afternoon
to an isolated ramshackle venta in a rocky wilderness. An enormous shaggy man of a zoölogical cast
of countenance, and a male-limbed girl were harnessing mules in the yard. No other living thing showed
itself. I offered a peseta for food. The man glared
at me for a time in silence, then growled that he
sold nothing, but that I should find a posada not far
beyond. He was evidently the champion prevari-
cator of that region, for not the suggestion of a hovel
appeared during the rest of the afternoon. But he
would be a fellow with Sancho indeed, who could not
overrule a few hour's appetite in thinking of higher
things, and no fit traveler in this hard, toilsome land

where overeating is not numbered among the vices.

The setting of the sun was perhaps an hour off when the highway, swinging a bit to the left and surmounting a barren, rocky ridge, laid suddenly before me an enthralling prospect. Below, far down on a distinctly lower level, a flat, ruffled country still misty with rising waves of heat, stretched away to the uttermost endless distance. The whole, glinting in the oblique rays of the setting sun, was scored in every direction with dull rock villages huddled compactly together, while on every hand, like signal fires on a western prairie, rose from a hundred threshing-floors columns of chaff straight and slender into the motionless air to an incredible height before breaking up. The road descended with decision, yet in no unseemly haste and, marching for an hour across a country traveled only by an occasional donkey loaded with chopped straw, led me at nightfall into the scene of Sancho's labors in the wheat-piles — the village of Tembleque.

In its immense fonda, but for the underground stables one single, vast, cobble-paved room, a vacant-eyed old man, a girl, and a leviathan of a woman sat among the carts, wine-casks, and heaps of harnesses, the latter knitting. In strictest Castilian the establishment was no fonda, but a *parador*, from *parar*, to stop; and certainly it could not with honesty have laid claim to any more inviting name, for assuredly no man in his senses would have dreamed of choosing it as a *staying*-place. When I asked if lodging was to be had, the woman replied with a caustic sneer that she had always been able thus far to accommodate any who were able and willing to pay.

" And can one also get supper? " I inquired timorously.

" How on earth do I know? " snapped the woman.

I stared with a puzzled air at the old man and he in like manner at the knitter, who turned out to be his wife, espoused in budding maidenhood when his march in life had well begun.

" How can I cook him supper if he has none with him? " snarled the no longer maidenly.

" Er — what have you brought to eat? " asked the preadamite in a quavering voice.

" Nothing to be sure. What is a fonda for? "

" Ah, then how can la señora mía get you supper? Over the way is the butcher, beyond, the green-grocer, further still the panadero —"

I returned some time later with meat, bread, potatoes, garbanzos, and a variety of vegetables, supplied with which the señora duly prepared me a supper — by sitting tight in her chair and issuing a volley of commands to the girl and the old man. For this service she demanded two " fat dogs," and collected at the same time an equal amount for my lodging.

When I had eaten, the mistress of the house

mumbled a word to the dotard. He lighted with
trembling hand a sort of miner's lamp and led the
way downward into the subterranean stable and for
what seemed little short of a half-mile through great
stone vaults musty with time, close by the cruppers
of an army of mules and burros. Opening at last a
door some three feet square and as many above the
floor, he motioned to me to climb through it into a
bin filled with chaff. This was to all appearances
clean, yet I hesitated. For in these endless vaults,
to which the outer air seemed not to have penetrated
for a century, it was cold as a November evening.
I glanced at the old man in protest. He blinked back
at me, shook his ever-quaking head a bit more
forcibly, and turning, shuffled away through the resounding cavern, the torch casting at first weird,
dancing shadows behind his wavering legs, then
gradually dying out entirely. I stood in blackest
darkness, undecided. Before, however, the last faint
sound of his going had wholly passed away, the
scrape of the veteran's faltering feet grew louder
again and in another moment he reappeared, clutching under one thin arm a heavy blanket. When I
had taken it, he put a finger to his lips, cast his
sunken eyes about him, whispered "sh!" with a
labored wink, and tottered once more away. I
climbed into the bin and slept soundly until the cursing of arrieros harnessing their mules aroused me
shortly before dawn.

A street

CHAPTER IX

THE TRAIL OF THE PRIEST

THE people of Tembleque had been just certain enough that none but an arriero could follow the intricate route thither, and that no man could cover the distance on foot in one day, to cause me to awaken determined to leave the Madrid highway and strike cross-country to Toledo. The first stage of the journey was the road to the village of Mora, which I was long in finding because at its entrance to — which chanced also to be its exit from — Tembleque it split up like an unraveled shoe-string. I got beyond the loose ends at last, however, and set a sharp pace — even though the hole in my shoe had enlarged to the size of a peseta — across a scarred and weather-beaten landscape that seemed constantly reminding how aged is the world.

Twenty-four kilometers brought me to Mora, a sturdy town of countrymen, in time for an early and stinted dinner and inquiries which led me off in a new direction up a steadily mounting region to Mascargne. There, at a still different point of the compass, a ruined castle on a hilltop ten kilometers away

was pointed out to me as the landmark of El Mona-
cail; to which village a rugged and sterile road clambered over a country hunch-backed with hills.   It was
siesta-time when I arrived, the sun scorching hot, a
burning wind sweeping among the patched and misshapen hovels that made up the place.   There were
no inhabitants abroad, which argued their good
sense; but in the shadow of the only public building
a trio of soldiers were playing at cards.   They leered
at me for some time when I made inquiry, then burst
out in derisive laughter.

" Claro, hombre! " answered one of them sarcastically.   " You can walk to Toledo la Santa if you
know enough to follow a cow-path."

I stumbled into it just beyond, a cow-path indeed,
though too little used to be clearly marked, and
meandering in and out with it for twenty kilometers
through rocky *barrancas* and across sandy patches,
gained as the day was nearing its close the wind-
bitten village of Nambroca.   A few miles more
through a still greater chaos of rocks and I came out
unexpectedly on the crest of a jagged promontory
that brought me to a sudden halt before one of the
most fascinating panoramas in all Spain.

A still higher rise cutting off the foreground, there
began a few miles beyond, the vast, wrinkled, verdureless plateau of Castile, rolling away and upward like
an enormous tilted profile-map of the world, sea-blue
with distance and heat rays, all details blended to-

gether into an indistinctness that left only an undivided impression like a Whistlerian painting. I pushed forward and at the top of the next ridge gasped aloud with new wonder. From this summit the world fell pell-mell away at my feet into a bottomless gorge; and beyond, two or three miles away, the culminating point in a tumultuous landscape of ravines, gulleys and precipitous chasms, sat an Oriental city, close-packed and isolated in its rocky solitude, the sun's last rays casting over its domes and minaret-like spires a flood of color that seemed suddenly and bodily to transport the beholder into the very heart of Asia. My goal was won; before me lay the ancient capital of the Goths, history-rich Toledo.

I sat down on the crest of the precipice overhanging the Tajo, almost beneath the enormous iron cross set in a rock to mark Toledo as the religious center of Spain, and remained watching the city across the gulf, full certain that whatever offered within its walls could in no degree equal the view from this facing hilltop. Richly indeed did this one sight of her reward the long day's tramp across the choking hills, even had there not been a pleasure in the walk itself; and upon me fell a great pity for those that come to her by railroad in the glare of day and the swelter of humanity.

As I sat, and the scene was melting away into the descending night, a voice sounded behind me and a ragged, slouching son of fortune proffered the accustomed greeting and, rolling a cigarette, sat down at my side. He was a " child of Toledo," and of his native city we fell to talking. At length he raised his flabby fist and, shaking it at the twinkling lights across the Tajo, cried out:

" O Toledo, my city! Gaunt, sunken-bellied Toledo, bound to your rock and devoured by the vulture horde of bloated churchmen while your children are starving!

" Señor," he continued, suddenly returning to a conversational tone, " let me show you but one of a thousand iniquities of these frailuchos."

He rose and led the way a little further along the path I had been following, halting at the edge of a yawning hole in the rocks, like a bottomless well, the existence of which I was thankful to have learned before I continued my way.

" Señor," he said, " no man can tell how many have died here, for it lies, as you see, in the very center of the trail over these hills. For a hundred years, as my grandfather has known, it has stood so. But do you think yon cursed priests would spend a perrito of their blood-sweated booty to cover it? "

It was black night when I picked my way down into the valley of the Tajo and, crossing the Alkántara bridge, climbed painfully upstairs into Toledo. Even within, the Oriental impression was not lost.

A wind-swept village

A bridge over the Tajo — Toledo

though the Castilian tongue sounded on every side. With each step forward came some new sign to recall that for half the past eight hundred years Toledo was an Arab-ruled and Arabic-speaking city. Thus it is still her Eastern fashion to conceal her wealth by building her houses inwardly, leaving for public thoroughfare the narrow, haphazard passageways between them, and giving to the arriving stranger the sensation of wandering through a haughty crowd of which each coldly turns his back.

Her medley of streets was such as one might find in removing the top of an ant-hill, an ant-hill in which modern improvements have made little progress; her pavements of round, century-polished cobble-stones, glinting in the weak light of an occasional street-lamp, were painful indeed to blistered feet. Ugly and barn-like outwardly, like the Alhambra, her houses frequently resemble that ancient palace, too, in that they are rich with decoration and comfort within. It was an hour or more before I was directed to a casa de huéspedes in the calle de la Lechuga, or Lettuce street, a gloomy crack between two rows of buildings. The house itself was such as only a man of courage would have entered by night in any other city. I ventured in, however, and found the family out-of-doors — lolling in the flower and palm-grown patio beneath the star-riddled sky, the canvas that formed the roof by day being drawn back. Even the well was in the patio, on which opened, like the others, the room to which I was assigned, presenting toward the street a blank, windowless wall.

It was late the next forenoon before I had slept the forty hot and rocky miles out of my legs and sallied forth to visit a shoemaker. As he lived only two streets away, it was my good fortune to find him in less than an hour, and as Toledo is the last city in the world in which a man would care to run about in his socks, I sat on a stool beside his workbench for something over three hours. His home and shop consisted of one cavernous room; his family, of a wife who sewed so incessantly that one might easily have fancied her run by machinery, and of a daughter of six who devised more amusement with a few scraps of leather than many another might with all the toys of Nürnberg. The shoemaker was of that old-fashioned tribe of careful workmen, taking pride in their labor, whom it is always a joy to meet — though not always to sit waiting for. He, too, hinted at the misery of life in Toledo, but unlike the specter of the night before, did not lay the blame for the sunken condition of his city on the " frailuchos," charging it rather to the well-known perverseness of fate, either because he was of an orthodox turn of mind or because his wife sat close at hand. When he had finished, having sewed soles and nailed heels on my shoes that were to endure until Spain was left behind, he collected a sum barely equal to forty cents.

In striking contrast to him — indeed, the two well

illustrated the two types of workmen the world harbors — was the barber who performed the next service. He was a mountain of sloth who rose with almost a growl at being disturbed and, his mind elsewhere, listlessly proceeded to the task before him. Though he was over forty and knew no other trade, he had not learned even this one, but haggled and clawed as that breed of man will who drifts through life without training himself to do anything. The reflective wanderer comes more and more to respect only the man, be he merely a street-sweeper, who does his life's work honestly; the "four-flusher" is ever a source of nausea and a lowerer of the tone of life, be he the president of a nation.

While I suffered, a priest dropped in to have his tonsure renovated and gloriously outdid in the scrofulousness of his anecdotes not only this clumsy wielder of the helmet of Mambrino, but exposed poor timorous Boccaccio for a prude and a Quaker.

Packed away down in a hollow of the congested city is that famous cathedral surnamed "la Rica." "The Rich"— it would be nearer justice to dub her the Midian, the Ostentatious, for she is so overburdened and top-heavy with wealth that one experiences at sight of her a feeling almost of disgust, as for a woman garish with jewelry. We of the United States must see, to conceive what shiploads of riches are heaped up within the churches of Spain by the superstitions of her people and the rapacity of her

priests, who, discovering the impossibility of laying
up their booty hereafter, agree with many groans to
stack it here.

"The Spanish church," observes Gautier, "is
scarcely any longer frequented except by tourists,
mendicants, and horrible old women." If one choose
the right hour of the afternoon even these vexations
are chiefly absent, entirely, perhaps, but for a poor
old crone or two kneeling before some mammoth doll
tricked out to represent the Virgin and bowing down
now and then in true Mohammedan fashion to kiss
the stone flagging. The Iberian traveler must visit
the cathedrals of the peninsula, not merely because
they offer the only cool retreat on a summer day, but
because they are the museums of Spain's art and
history. But even the splendor of the setting sun
through her marvelous stained-glass windows cannot
overcome the oppressiveness of "la Rica."

As he stands before the wondrous paintings that
enrich the great religious edifices of Spain, the mat-
ter-of-fact American of to-day is not unlikely to be
assailed by other thoughts than the pure esthetic.
There comes, perhaps, the reflection of how false is
that oft-repeated assertion that the world's truly great
artists exercised their genius solely for pure art's
sake. Would they then have prostituted their years
on earth to tickling the vanity of their patrons, in
depicting the wife of some rich candle-maker walking arm in arm with the Nazarene on the Mount of

" Toledo la rica "

Olives, or the absurdity of picturing Saint Fulano, who was fed to Roman lions in A. D. 300, strolling through a Sevillian garden with the infant Jesus in his arms and a heavenly smirk on his countenance? How much greater treasures might we have to-day had they thrown off the double yoke of contemporaneous superstitions and servility to wealth and painted, for example, the real Mary as in their creative souls they saw her, the simple Jewish housewife amid her plain Syrian surroundings. Instead of which they have set on canvas and ask us to accept as their real conception voluptuous-faced "Virgins" who were certainly painted from models of a very different type, and into whose likeness in spite of the painter's skill has crept a hint that the poser's thoughts during the sitting were much less on her assumed motherhood of a deity than on the coming evening's amours.

Horror, too, stands boldly forth in Spanish painting. The Spaniard is, incongruously enough, a realist of the first water. He will see things materially, graphically; the bullfight is his great delight, not the pretended reality of the theater. Centuries of fighting the infidel, centuries of courting self-sacrifice in slaying heretics, the reaction against the sensuous gentleness of the Moor, have all combined to make his Christianity fervid, savage, sanguinary. Yielding to which characteristic of his fellow-countrymen, or tainted with it himself, many

a Spanish artist seems to have gloried in depicting
in all gruesome detail martyrs undergoing torture,
limbs and breasts lopped off and lying bleeding close
at hand, unshaven torturers wielding their dripping
knives with fiendish merriment. These horrors, too,
are set up in public places of worship, where little
children come daily, and even men on occasion. It
is strange, indeed, if childhood's proneness to imitation does not make the playground frequently the
scene of similar martyrdoms. How much better to
treat the tots to a daily visit to the morgue, where
what they see would at least be true to nature — and
far less repulsive.

There are other " sights " in Toledo than the
cathedral for him who is successful in running them
down in her jungle of streets. Each such chase is
certain sooner or later to bring him out into the
Zocodover, that disheveled central plaza in which the
sunbeams fall like a shower of arrows. The inferno
into which he seems plunged unwarned chokes at
once the rambler's grumble at the intricacies of the
city and brings him instead to mumble praises of the
Arabs, who had the good sense so to build that the
sun with his best endeavors rarely gets a peep into the
depth of the pavement; and the time is short indeed
before he dives back into the relief of one of the radi-
ating calles.

As often as I crossed the " Zoco " my eyes were
drawn to a ragged fellow of my own age, with a six-

The sun-dodging streets of Toledo

inch stump for one leg, lolling prone on the dirt-carpeted earth in a corner of the square, mumbling from time to time over his cigarette:

" Una limosnita, señores; qué Dios se lo pagará."

There was in his face evidence that he had been born with fully average gifts, perhaps special talents; and a sensation of sadness mingled with anger came upon me with the reflection that through all the years I had been living and learning and journeying to and fro upon the earth, this hapless fellow-mortal had been squatting in the dust of Toledo's Zocodover, droning the national lamentation:

" A little alms, señores, and may God repay you."

Just another was he of her thousands of sons that Spain has wantonly let go to waste, until even at this early age he had sunk to a lump of living human carrion that all the powers of earth or from Elsewhere could not remake into the semblance of a man.

Try though one may, one cannot escape the conviction that the fat of Toledo goes to the priesthood, both physically and figuratively. High or low, the churchmen that overrun the place have all a sleek, contented air and on their cynical, sordid faces an all too plain proof of addiction to the flesh pots; while the layman has always a hungry look, not quite always of animal hunger for food, but at least for those things that stand next above. Nowhere can one escape the cloth. Every half-hour one is sure to run across at least a bishop tottering under a fortune's-worth of robes and attended by a bodyguard of acolytes, pausing now and again to shed his putative blessing on some devout passer-by. Of lesser dignitaries, of cowled monks and religious mendicants there is no lack, while with the common or garden variety of priest, a cigarette hanging from a corner of his mouth, his shovel hat set at a rakish angle, his black gown swinging with the jauntiness of a stage Mephistopheles, ogling the girls in street or promenade, the city swarms. Distressingly close is the resemblance of these latter to those creatures one may find loitering about the stage-door toward the termination of a musical comedy.

I sat one afternoon on a bench of that broken promenade that partly surrounds Toledo high above the Tajo, watching the sun set across the western vega, when my thoughts were suddenly snatched back through fully a thousand years of time by the six-o'clock whistle of the Fabrica de Armas below. When my astonishment had died away, there came over me the recollection that not once before in all Spain had I heard that sound, a factory whistle. Agreeable as that absence of sibilant discord is to the wanderer's soul, I could not but wonder whether just there is not the outward mark of one of the chief reasons why the Spain of to-day straggles where she does in the procession of nations.

I descended one afternoon from Lettuce street to

the sand-clouded station on the plain and spent the
ensuing night in Aranjuéz, a modern checker-board
city planted with exotic elms and royal palaces.   It
was again afternoon before I turned out into the
broad highway that, crossing the Tajo, struck off
with business-like directness across a vega fertile
with wheat.   Before long it swung sharply to the
right and, laboring up the scarified face of a cliff,
gained the great central tableland of Castilla Nueva,
then stalked away across a weird and solemn landscape as drear and desolate as the hills of Judea.

The crabbed village that I fell upon at dusk furnished me bread and wine, but no lodging.   I plodded
on, trusting soon to find a more hospitable hamlet.
But the desolation increased with the night; neither
man nor habitation appeared.   Toward eleven I gave
up the search and, stepping off the edge of the highway, found a bit of space unencumbered with rocks
and lay down until the dawn.

. The sun rose murky.   In twenty kilometers the
deserted carretera passed only two squalid wine-
shops.   Then rounding in mid-morning a slight eminence, it presented suddenly to my eyes a smoky, indistinct, yet vast city stretching on a higher plane
half across the desolate horizon.   It was Madrid.
I tramped hours longer, so uncertainly did the
highway wander to and fro seeking an entrance,
but came at last into a miserable outskirt village and tossed away the stick that had borne my

knapsack since the day I had fashioned that convenience in the southern foothills of Andalusia. Two besmirched street Arabs, pouncing upon it almost as it fell — so extraordinary a curiosity was it in this unwooded region — waged pitched battle until each carried away a half triumphant.   I pushed on across the massive Puente de Toledo high above the trickle of water that goes by the name of the river Manzanares and, mounting through a city as different from Toledo as Cairo from Damascus, halted at last in the mildly animated Puerta del Sol, the center of Spain and, to the Spaniard, of the universe.

La Puerta del Sol, Madrid: the Spaniard's center of the universe

CHAPTER X

A DAY or two later I was installed for a fortnight in a casa de huéspedes in the calle San
Bernardo. In such places as one plans to remain
for any length of time there are few cheaper ar-
rangements for ample fare in all Europe than these
Spanish " houses of guests." My room, which was
temporarily on the second-floor front, but solemnly
pledged to be soon changed to the third-floor back,
was all that an unpampered wanderer could have required. Breakfast was light; a cup of chocolate and
a roll — no self-respecting traveler ventures to
sample Spanish coffee more than once. But one
soon grows accustomed and indeed to prefer the
European abstemiousness at the first meal. In compensation the *almuerzo* and *comida*, at twelve and
seven, were more than abundant. A thick soup,
not unseldom redolent of garlic, was followed by a
salad, and that by a *puchero*, which is to say an
entire meal on one platter,— in the center a square
of boiled beef flanked like St. Peter's amid the hills of
Rome by seven varieties of vegetables, the *garban-*

zos — bright yellow chickpeas of the size of marbles — with the usual disproportion granted that robust comestible in Spain, overtowering not only every other eminence but carpeting the intervening valleys. That despatched, or seriously disfigured, there came a second offering from the animal world, — a *cocido* or an *olla podrida,* after which the repast descended gradually by fruit, cheese, and cigarettes to its termination. Through it all a common wine flowed generously.

Even on Friday this sturdy good cheer knew no abatement. Centuries ago, in the raging days of the Moor, the faithful of Spain were granted for their Catholic zeal and bodily behoof this dispensasation, that they might nourish their lean frames on whatever it should please Santiago, their patron, to bring within bowshot of their home-made crosspieces. The Moor has long since removed his dusky shadow from the land, but the dispensation remains. Indeed, there is left scarcely a custom the inobservance of which betrays the non-Catholic; or if one there be at all general it is this: when he yawns — which he is not unwont to do even at table — the devout Spaniard makes over his mouth the sign of the cross, to keep the devil from gaining a foothold therein — an exorcism that is not always successful.

There is yet another custom, quite the opposite of religious in result at least, which the guest at a casa de huéspedes must school himself to endure. It

The Manzanares, Madrid's only river

grows out of the Spaniard's infernal politeness.
Figure to yourself that you have just returned from
a morning of tramping through sweltering Madrid
on the ephemeral breakfast already noted, and sit
down at table just as a steaming puchero is served.
With a melodious and self-sacrificing " Serve yourself, señor," the addle-pated Spaniard across the
way pushes the dish to his neighbor; to which the
neighbor responds by pushing it back again with a
" No! Serve *yourself*, señor," followed in quick succession by " No! No! Serve yourself, señor; " " No!
No! No! señor! Serve yourself! " " No! No! No!
No! serve —" and so on to the end of time, or until
a wrathy Anglo-Saxon, rising in his place, picks up
the source of dispute and establishes order.

Our household in the calle San Bernardo consisted
of a lawyer, a " man of affairs "— using the latter word in its widest signification — of two young
Germans, " Don Hermann " and " Don Ricardo,"
for some time employed in the city, and of the family
itself. Of this the husband, a slouching, toothless
fellow of fifty, and the grandmother were mere
supernumeraries. The speaking parts were taken by
the wife and daughter, the former an enormous,
unpolished woman with a well-developed mustache and the over-developed voice of a stevedore.
Indeed, a stentorian, grating voice and a habit of
speaking always at the tiptop of it is one of the
chief afflictions of the Spanish women of the masses

— and of their hearers. Is it by chance due to the custom of studying and reciting always aloud and in chorus during their few years of schooling? Quién sabe? There was presented during my stay in Madrid the play, or more properly playlet — zarzuela — " Levantar Mueros — Raising the Dead "; but I dared not go lest it turn out to be a dramatized sewing circle.

But it remains to introduce the star member of the cast, the center of that San Bernardo universe around which revolved mother, supernumeraries, and guests like planets in their orbits — the daughter. I fully expect to wander many a weary mile before I again behold so beautiful a maid — or one that I should take more pleasure in being a long way distant from. She was sixteen — which in Spain is past childhood — a glorious, faultless blonde in a land where blondes are at high premium, her lips forming what the Spaniard calls a " nido de besos "— a nest of osculatory delights — and — But why drive the impossible task further? Such radiant perfections in human form must be seen at least to be appreciated. It is sufficient, perhaps, to mention that her likeness was on sale in every novelty shop in Madrid and found more purchasers than that of Machaquito, King of the Toreros. In short, a supreme beauty — had she been captured early and suitably polished instead of remaining at home with mother until she had acquired mother's voice, and mother's roughshod manners, and a slothful habit of life that was destined, alas, in all probability to end by reproducing her mother's bulk and mustache.

There are two things worth seeing in howling, meeowling, brawling, blistering Madrid — her outdoor life and the Prado museum. It was the latter that I viewed by day, for when relentless August has settled down the capital is not merely hot, it is plutonic, cowering under a dead, sultry heat without the relief of a breath of air, a heat that weighs down like a leaden blanket and makes Seville seem by comparison a northern seaport. A saying as old as its foolish founder's grave credits the city with three month's invierno and nine months' infierno, a characterization that loses much in symmetry, though gaining, perhaps, in force by translation. It was my fortune to have happened into the place when the lowest circle of the latter region was having its inning.

Wherefore I went often to the Prado; and came as often away more physically fatigued than after a four-hour watch in a stokehole, and with my head in a bewildered whirl that even a long stroll in the Buen Retiro only partly reduced. It is like the irrationality of man to bring together these thousands of masterpieces, so close together that not one of them can produce a tenth of its proper effect. Of the pictures in the Prado the seeing alone would require two years of continuous work, the attempt to describe, a lifetime; pictures running through all the gamut of art from the fading of the pre-Raphaelites down to Goya, that plain-spoken Goya who seems to have stood afar off and thrown paint by the bucketful at his canvas — with marvelous results. A pandemonium of paintings, not one of which but off by itself would bring daily inspiration to all beholders. It is the tendency of all things to crowd together — wealth, art, learning, work, leisure, poverty; man's duty to combat this tendency by working for a sane and equitable distribution. The Prado collection would be a treasure, indeed, had those who exerted themselves to bring these paintings together given half that exertion to spreading them out. Then it might be that in a land as rich with art as Spain one would not find daubs and beer-calendars hung in the place of honor in the homes and fondas of " the masses." When the good day comes that the accumulation of the Prado is dispersed I shall bespeak as my share the " Borrachos " or " Vulcan's Forge " of sturdy Velazquez.

Those who are curious may also visit, at seasons and with permissions, the unpleasing royal palace, about the outer walls of which sleep scores of fly-proof vagrants in the shade of half leafless trees, and sundry other government buildings, all of which — except the vagrants — are duly and fully described in the guide-books. There is, too, the daily *Juego de Pelota,* imported from the Basque prov-

"Los borrachos."—Velasquez

inces, a sort of enlarged handball played in a slate-
walled chamber in which the screaming of gamblers
for bids and their insults to the players know no ces-
sation. Wandering aimlessly through her streets, as
the sojourner in Madrid must who cannot daily sleep
the day through, I found myself often pausing to
admire the splendid displays in the windows of her
tailors. Spain has no wool schedule, and as I gazed
a deep regret came over me that I could not always
be a dweller in Madrid when my garb grows thread-
bare or a tailor bill falls due. But there was sure
remedy for such melancholy. When it grew acute
I had but to turn and note the fitting of these
splendid fabrics on the passer-by, and the sadness
changed to a wonder that the madrileño tailor has
the audacity to charge at all for his services.

So bare and uninviting are her environs — and she
has no suburbs — that Madrid never retires outwardly as other cities for her picnics and holidays,
but crowds more closely together in the Buen Retiro.
The congestion is greatest about the Estanque
Grande. The largest body of water the normal
madrileño ever sees is this artificial pond of about the
area — though not the depth — of a college swim-
ming-pool. On it are marooned a few venerable
rowboats, for a ride in which most of the residents of
Madrid have been politely quarreling every fair day
since they reached a quarrelsome age. Small wonder
dwellers in the capital cry out in horror at the idea

of drinking water. One might as sanely talk of
burning wood for fuel.

Obviously no untraveled native of "las Cortes"
has more than a vague conception of the sea. Indeed, the ignorance on this point is nothing short
of pathetic, if one may judge from the popular sea
novel that fell into my hands during my stay. The
writer evidently dwelt in the usual hotbox that consti-
tutes a Madrid lodging and had not the remotest,
wildest notion what thing a sea may be, nor the
ability to tell a mainsail from a missionary's mule.
But he was a clever man — to have concocted such a
yarn and escaped persecution.

Madrid, however, like all urban Spain, comes
thoroughly to life only with the fall of night. Oc-
casionally a special celebration carries her populace
to some strange corner of the city, but the fixed
rendezvous is the Paseo de Recoletos, a broader Alameda where reigns by day an un-Spanish opulence
of shade enjoyed only by the chairs stacked house-
high beneath the trees. There is nothing hurried
about the congregating. Dinner leisurely finished,
the madrileño of high or low degree begins to drift
slowly thither. By nine the public benches are taken;
by ten one can and must move only with the throng
at the accepted pace, or pay a copper to sit in
haughty state in one of the now unstacked chairs.
Toward ten-thirty a military band straggles in from
the four points of the compass, finishes its cigarette,

languidly unlimbers its instruments, and near eleven falls to work — or play. About the same time there come wandering through the trees, as if drawn here by merest chance, five threadbare blind men, each with a battered violin or horn tucked tenderly under one arm. During the opening number they listen attentively, in silence, after the manner of musicians. Then as the official players pause to roll new cigarettes the sightless ragamuffins take their stand near at hand and strike up a music that more than one city of the western world could do worse than subsidize. Thereafter melody is incessant; and with it the murmur of countless voices, the scrape of leisurely feet on the gravel, the cries of the hawkers of all that may by any chance be sought, and louder and more insistent than all else the baying of newsboys — aged forty to sixty and of both sexes —" *El País!* " " *El Heraldo!* " " *La Cor-r-respondencia-a-a-a!* "

Midnight! Why, midnight is only late in the afternoon in Madrid. The concert does not end until three and half the babies of the city are playing in the sand along the Paseo de Recoletos when the musicians leave. Besides, what else is to be done? Even did one feel the slightest desire to turn in there is not the remotest possibility of finding one's room less than a sweatbox. The populace shows little inclination to disperse, and though many saunter unwillingly homeward for form's sake, it is not to sleep, for one may still hear chatting and the muffled twang of guitars behind the blinds of the open windows. As for myself, I drifted commonly after the concert into the " Circo Americano " or a zarzuela, though such entertainments demonstrated nothing except how easily the madrileño is amused. Yet even these close early — for Madrid; and rambling gradually into my adopted section, it was usually my fortune to run across a " friend of the house "— of whom more anon — to retire with him to the nearest *Juego de Billar*, or billiard-hall, there to play the night gray-headed.

The doors of Madrid close at midnight, and neither the madrileño nor his guests have yet reached that stage of civilization where they can be entrusted with their own latch-key. But it is easy for all that to gain admittance. One has only to halt before one's door, clap one's hands soundly three or six or nine or fifteen times, bawl in one's most musical and topmost voice, " Ser-r-r-r-reno! " not forgetting to roll the r like the whir of a broken emery-wheel, and then sit calmly down on the curb and wait. Within a half-hour, or an hour at most, the watchman is almost sure to appear, rattling with gigantic keys, carrying staff and lantern, and greeting the exile with all the compliments of the Spanish season, unlocks, furnishes him a lighted wax taper, wishes him a " good night " and a long day's sleep, and gracefully pockets his two-cent fee.

Theoretically the sereno is supposed to keep order

An Alameda by day — chairs stacked until busy night-time

— or at least orderly. But nothing is more noted for its absence in Madrid by night than order. The sereno of the calle San Bernardo showed great liking for the immediate neighborhood of our casa de huéspedes — after I had been admitted. Rare the night — that is, morning — that he did not sit down beneath my window — for my promotion to the third-floor back was postponed until I left the city — with a pair of hackmen or day-hawks and fall to rehearsing in a foghorn-voice the story of his noble past. Twice or thrice I let drop a hint in the form of what water was in my pitcher. But the serenos of Madrid are imperturbable, and water is precious. On each such occasion the romancer moved over some two feet and serenely continued his tale until the rising sun sent him strolling homeward.

"Don Ricardo," of our German boarders, aspired to change from his stool in a banking-house to the bullring. He had taken a course in Madrid's Escuela Taurina and was already testing his prowess each Sunday as a banderillero in the little plaza of Tetuan, a few miles outside the city. In consequence — for "Ricardo" was a companionable youth for all his ragged Spanish — our casa de huéspedes became a rendezvous of lesser lights in the taurine world. Two or three toreros were sure to drop in each evening before we had sipped the last of our wine, to spend an hour or two in informal *tertulia*. I had not been a week in the city before I numbered among my acquaintances Curdito, Capita de Carmona, Pepete, and Moreno de Alcalá, all men whose names have decorated many a ringside poster.

There appeared one evening among the "friends of the house" a young man of twenty, of singularly attractive appearance and personality. Clear-eyed, of lithe yet muscular frame, and a spring-like quickness in every movement, he was noticeable above all for his modest deportment, having barely a touch of that arrogant self-esteem that is so frequently the dominating characteristic of the Spaniard. His speech was the soft, musical Andalusian; his conversation quickly demonstrated him a man of a high rate of intelligence.

Such was Faustino Posadas, bullfighter, already a favorite among the aficionados of Spain, though it is by no means often that a youth of twenty finds himself vested with the red muleta. Son of the spare-limbed old herder who has been keeper for many years of the Tabladas, or bull pastures, of Seville, he had been familiar with the animals and their ways from early childhood. At sixteen he was already a banderillero. A famous espada carried him in his caudrilla to Peru and an accident to a fellow torero gave him the opportunity to despatch his first two bulls in the plaza of Lima. He returned to Spain a full-fledged "novillero" and was rapidly advancing to the rank of graduate espada, with the right to appear before bulls of any age.

Once introduced, Posadas appeared often in the calle San Bernardo; much too often in fact to leave any suspicion that either his frendship for "Don Ricardo " or the charms of our conversation was the chief cause of his coming. A very few days passed before it had become a fixed and accepted custom for him to set out toward nine for the Paseo with the radiant daughter of the house — though mother waddled between, of course, after the dictates of Spanish etiquette. Within a week he was received by the family on the footing of a declared suitor; and of his favor with the señorita there was no room for doubt.

There was always a long hour between the termination of supper and the time when Madrid began its nightly promenade, during which it was natural that our conversation should touch chiefly upon affairs of the ring.

"Don Henrico," asked Capita one evening — for I was known to the company as " Henrico Franco "—" is it true that there are no bullfights in your country? "

"Vaya que gente! " burst out Moreno, when I had at length succeeded in making clear to them our national objections to the sport. " What rubbish! What does it matter if a few old hacks that would soon fall dead of themselves are killed to make sport for the aficionados? As for the bull — Carajo, hombre! You yourself, if you were in such a rage as the toro, would no more feel the thrust of a sword than the pricking of a gadfly."

Posadas, on the other hand, readily grasped the American point of view. He even admitted that he found the goring of the horses unpleasant and that he would gladly see that feature of the córrida eliminated if there were any other way of tiring the bull before the last act. But for the bull himself he professed no sympathy whatever.

"What would you have us do?" he cried in conclusion. "Spain offers nothing else for a son of the people without political pull than to become torero. Without that we must work as peasants on black bread and a peseta a day."

"As in any other trade," I inquired, "I suppose you enter the ring without any thought of danger, any feeling of fear?"

"No, I don't remember ever being afraid," laughed the Sevillian, "though when Miúra furnishes the stock I like to hear mass before the córrida."

"What are the secrets of success?"

"I know only one," answered Posadas, "and that is no secret. Every move the bull makes shows first in the whites of his eyes. Never for an instant do I take my eyes off his. So it has been my luck not to be once wounded," he concluded, making the sign of the cross.

" Cogidas! " cried Capita, passing a hand over a dull brown welt on his neck. " Caramba! I have five of them, and every one by a cursed miúra. No, I never felt pain, only a cold chill that runs down to your very toes. But afterward — in the hospital! Carajo! "

One would suppose that men engaged in so perilous a calling would take extreme bodily care of themselves. Not a torero among them, however, knew the meaning of " training " as the word is used by our athletes. They drank, smoked — even during the córrida — ate what and when they pleased, and more commonly spent the night strolling in the Paseo with an " amiga " or carousing in a wineshop than sleeping. Whether it is a leaving of the Moor or native to this blear, rocky land, there is much of the fatalist in the Spaniard, especially the Andalusian. He is by nature a gambler; be he torero, beggar, or senator, he is always ready and willing to " take a chance."

" If a man is marked to be killed in the ring he will be killed there," asserted Pepete. " He cannot change his fate by robbing himself of the pleasures of life."

Posadas was engaged to appear in the plaza of Madrid on the first Sunday of our acquaintance. When I descended to the street at three the city was already drifting ringward, a picador in full trim now and then cantering by on his Rozinante — a sight fully as exciting to the populace as the circus parade of our own land. I had reached the edge of the Puerta del Sol when I heard a " Hóla, amigo ! " behind me and turning, beheld none other than Jesús the Sevillian bearing down upon me with outstretched hand. He had found work at his trade in the city — though not yet a barber apparently.

" And Gásparo ? " I asked.

" Perdido, señor ! Lost again ! " he sighed. " Perhaps he has found a new amiga. But I much more fear he has fallen into the fingers of the police. Mira V., señor. In all the journey we have not been able once to hide ourselves on a freight train. At last, señor, in Castillejo, Gásparo goes mad and swears he will ride once for nothing. With twenty people looking on he climbs a wagon. A man shouts ' thief ! ' and around the station comes running a guardia civil. I have not been able to find Gásparo since. Señor, I have come to think it is not right to ride on the railroad without a ticket. Gásparo, perhaps, is in prison. But we will meet again when he comes out," he concluded cheerfully, as I turned away.

At the plaza fully twelve thousand were gathered. The córrida was distinguished particularly for its clumsiness, though the fighters, while young, were not without reputation. Falls and bruises were

innumerable and the entire performance a chapter
of accidents that kept the aficionados in an uproar
and gave no small amount of work to the attendant
surgeons. Of the three matadores, Serenito, a
hulking fellow whose place seemed last of all in
the bullring, was gored across the loins by his first
bull and forced to abandon his task and fee to the
sobresaliente. Then Platerito —" Silver-plated "—
a mere whisp of a man, having dedicated to the populace as is the custom in Madrid the death of the fifth
bull, gasconaded up to the animal, fell immediately
foul of a horn, whirled about like a rag caught on
a fly-wheel, and landed on his shoulders fully sixty
feet away. To the astonishment even of the aficionados he sprang to his feet as jaunty as ever and duly
despatched the animal, though not over handily.

The misfortunes of his fellows served to bring out
by contrast the skill of Posadas. Not only did he
pass the day unscathed, but killed both his bulls at
the first thrust so instantly that the thud of their fall
might be heard outside the plaza, how rare a feat
only he knows who has watched the hacking and
butchering of many a "novillero." Indeed, so
pleasing was his work that he was at once engaged,
contrary to all precedent, to appear again on the
ensuing Sunday.

By that time I had learned enough of the " fine
points of the game " to recognize that the Sevillian
was approaching already true matador " form,"

and as I took leave of him next day it was with the conviction that success in his chosen career was as sure as the certainty of soon winning his most cherished reward.

"Vaya, Don Henrico," he laughed as we shook hands. "We shall see each other again. Some day when I go to Mexico or the Americas of the south I shall come by New York and you shall show me all you have told us of."

There are few countries in which it is more difficult to lay out an itinerary that will take in the principal points of interest without often doubling on one's track than Spain. By dint of long calculation and nice adjustment of details I sketched a labyrinthian route that my kilometer-book, together with what walking I should have time for, would cover. As for my check-book there was left exactly three pesetas a day for the remainder of my time in the peninsula.

So one cloudy morning in early August I took train at the Estación del Norte and wound away upward through the gorges of the Guardarrama to Segovia. Only there did I realize that the rumble of Madrid had been absolutely incessant in my ears; the stillness of the ancient city was almost oppressive, even more than in Toledo one felt peculiarly out of the world and a sensation that he must not remain too long lest he be wholly forgotten and lose his place in life's procession.

Faustino Posadas

A Spanish city's water-supply

In the morning I set off by the highway that follows for some miles the great unmortared aqueduct, that chief feature of Segovia, a thing indeed far greater than the town, as if a man's gullet, or his thirst should be larger than himself, so difficult is it for a city to obtain water in this thirsty land. Where the road abandoned the monument it continued across a country brown and sear, with almost the aspect of an American meadow in autumn, steadily rising all but imperceptibly. Well on in the morning I entered a forest, at a side road of which I was joined by two guardias civiles, who marched for an hour with me exchanging information and marveling that I had wandered so far afield. It has been my lot to become well, nay, intimately acquainted with the police of many lands, and I know of none that, as a body, are more nearly what police should be than these civil guards of Spain, to whom is due the suppression of all the old picturesque insecurities of the road. They have neither the bully-ism of our own club-wielders nor the childishness of Asiatic officers. Except in blistering Bailen the bearing of every pair I met — they never travel singly — was such as to win at once the confidence of the stranger and to draw out of him such facts as it is their duty to learn so naturally that it seemed but a mutual exchange of politenesses. There are, no doubt, petty corruptions in so large a body, but in the presence of almost any of them one has a conviction that their first thought is their duty.

The highway ended its climb at noon in La Granja — The Grange — residence of the king in spring and autumn, a town little Spanish in aspect seated in a carefully cropped forest at the base of a thickly wooded mountain. I roamed unchallenged for half the afternoon through the royal park, replete with fountains compared with which those of Versailles are mere water-squirts; playthings that Philip the half-mad accused of costing three million and amusing him three minutes. I was more fortunate, for they cost me nothing and amused me fully half an hour.

After which I picked up the highway again and, winding around the regal village, struck upward into the mountains of Guardarrama. At the hamlet of Valsain I had just paused at the public spring when the third or fourth tramp I had seen on the road in all Spain swung around a bend ahead, marching doggedly northward. As I stooped to drink, a moan and a thud sounded behind me. I turned quickly around to behold the roadster writhing in the middle of the highway, the gravel of which had cut and gashed one side of his face. The simple villagers, swarming wide-eyed out of their houses, would have it at first that he was my companion and I to blame for his mishap. He bore patent signs of months on the road, being burned a tawny brown in garb and face by the sun that was evidently the author of his misfortune. For a time the village stood open-mouthed about him, the brawny house-wives now and then giving vent to their sympathy and helpless perplexity by a long-drawn " ay de mi! " I suggested water, and a dozen women, dashing away with the agility of middle-aged cows, brought it in such abundance that the victim was all but drenched to the skin before I could drive them off. He revived a bit and while a woman clumsily washed the blood and gravel from his face, I addressed him in all the languages I could muster, for he was evidently no Spaniard. The only response was a few inarticulate groans, and when he had been carried to a grassy slope in the shade, I went on, knowing him in kind if awkward hands.

A half-perpendicular hour passed by, and I seemed to have left Spain behind. The road was toiling sharply upward through deep forests of evergreen, cool as an Alpine valley, opening now and then to offer a vista of thick treetops and a glimpse of red-tiled villages; a scene as different from sterile, colorless, sunken-cheeked Castille as could well be imagined. Nor did the dusk descend so swiftly in these upper heights. The sun had set when I reached the summit at six thousand feet and, passing through the Puerto de Navacerrada, started swiftly downward in the thickening gloom;

but it was some time before the night had settled
down in earnest.

I had marched well into it when I was suddenly
startled by a sound of muffled voices out of the
darkness ahead. I moved forward noiselessly, for
this lonely pass has many a story to tell. A dim
light shone through what appeared to be a window.
I shouted for admittance and a moment later found
myself in the hovel of a peon caminero.

Within, besides the family, were two educated
Spaniards, one indeed who had been a secretary in
the American Legation up to the outbreak of the
recent war. When he had been apprised of my
mode of travel and my goal, he stared wonderingly
at me for a moment and then stepped out with me
into the night. Marching a few paces down the
highway until we had rounded some obstruction, he
pointed away into the void.

" Do you see those lights? " he asked.

Far away and to the right, so far and so high
in the heavens that they seemed constellations,
twinkled three clusters of lights, almost in a row
but far separated one from another.

" The third and farthest," said my companion,
" is El Escorial; and your time is well-chosen, for
to-morrow is the day of Saint Lawrence, her patron
saint."

We returned to the hut, where the wife of the peon
was moved to cook me a bowl of garbanzos and

Mesh bridge and little river, Madrid

spread me a blanket on the stone floor. In the morning the sharply descending highway carried me quickly down the mountain, and by sunrise I was back once more in the familiar Castille. It was verging on noon when, surmounting a sterile rise, I caught sight of the dome and towers of the Escorial. A roadside stream, of which the water was lukewarm, removed the grim of travel, and I climbed sweltering into the village of Escorial de Arriba, pitched on a jagged shoulder of the calcined mountain high above the monastery.

Spain is wont to show her originality and indifference to the convenience of travelers, and on this, the anniversary of the grilling of him in whose honor it was built, the great monastery was closed for the only time during the year. I experienced no regret, however, for the vast gloomy structure against its background of barren, rocky hills had far too much the aspect of some dank prison to awaken any desire to enter. Least impressive of famous buildings, the Escorial is certainly the most oppressive. There is poetry, inspiration in many a building, in the Taj Mahal, the Cathedral of Cologne; but not in the Escorial. It suggests some frowning, bulky bourgeois of forty whose mother thinks him and who would fain believe himself one of the most poetic and spiritual of men.

I wandered away the day in the town, drifting in the afternoon down into the village " de Abajo."

13

There, in the multitude about the stone-pile of a bullring, I ran across Curdito in festive garb. He was scheduled to kill all three bulls of the day's córrida, but in spite of his urgent invitation I felt in no mood to sit out the blistering afternoon on a bare stone slab of this rough-and-tumble plaza.

El Escorial was so overrun with visitors to her annual celebration that not a lodging of any sort was to be had in either the upper or the lower village. The discovery brought me no shock, for a night out of doors I neither dreaded nor regretted. But as I sauntered at dusk down past the great building into the flanking "woods of Herrera," I could not but wonder how those travelers who bewail the accommodations of the "only possible hotel" would have met the situation.

Behind the monastery extends a broad, silent forest, not over thick, and beneath the trees squat bushes and brown heather. I spread the day's copy of the *Heraldo* between two shrubs and, stretching out at my ease, fell to munching the lunch I had bought in the village market. Let the circumstances be right and I know few more genuine joys than to sleep the night out of doors. Lie down in the open while a bit of daylight still lingers, or awaken there when the dawn has come, and there is a feeling of sordidness, mixed with the ludicrous, a sense of being an outcast prone on the common earth. But while the night, obscuring all details, hangs its canopy over the world there are few situations more pleasing.

When I had listened a while to the panting of the August night I fell asleep. For weeks past I had been viewing too many famous spots, perhaps, had been delving too constantly into the story of Spain. My constant use of Castilian, too, had borne fruit; English words no longer intruded even on my inner meditations. Was it possible also that the market lunch had been too heavy, or the nearness of the gloomy monastery too oppressive? At any rate I fell to dreaming.

At first there passed a procession of all Spain, — arrieros, peasants, Andalusian maidens, toreros, priests, Jesús the tramp, a chanting water-seller, merchants and beggars; close followed by two guardias civiles who looked at me intently as they passed. Then suddenly in their place Moors of every garb and size were dancing about me. They seemed to be celebrating a victory and to be preparing for some Mohammedan sacrifice. A mullah advanced upon me, clutching a knife. I started to my feet, a distant bell boomed heavily, and the throng vanished like a puff of smoke.

Away off above, in a hollow in the gaunt mountain, I made out gradually the form of a man sitting pensive, elbows on knees, gazing dark-browed down upon me. He was in royal robes, and all at once he seemed to start, to grow in size,

and a line across his breast expanded to the letters
"Felipe II." Larger and larger he grew until he
overtowered the mountain itself; then slowly,
scowlingly he rose and strode down upon me. A
women joined him, a scrawny woman who laid a
hand inertly in his, and I recognized Bloody Mary,
who seemed thus in an instant to have leaped over
the seas from her island kingdom to join her gloomy
husband.

In rapid succession new figures appeared,—
Herrera first, a torpid, lugubrious man strangely
like the building he has left behind; then quickly
a multitude, through which strolled a man whose
crown bore the name " Pedro," running his sword
with a chuckle of devilish laughter through any
that came within easy reach, young or old, asleep
or awake. Of a sudden there stalked forth from
nowhere a lean, deep-eyed man of fifty, a huge
parchment volume under one arm, an almost cynical, yet indulgent smile on his countenance; and
as if to prove who he was there raced down over
the mountain a man not unlike him in appearance,
astride a caricature of a horse, and behind him a
dumpy, wondering peasant ambling on an ass. The
cavalier sprang suddenly from his hack and fell
affectionately on the shoulder of the parchment-
bearer, then bounding back into the saddle he
charged straight for Felipe, who, stepping to one

Much bridge and little river—Madrid

The Escorial

A rural mail-carrier

side, flung, backhanded, Mary his wife far out of sight over the mountain.

A sound drew my attention to another side. Across the plain was marching with stately tread a long file of Moors, each carrying in one hand his head, by the hair.

"Los Abencerrajes!" I seemed to shout; and almost before it was uttered there remained only Felipe and behind him a score of indistinct forms. He waved a hand toward me and turned his back, and the company moved down upon me unlimbering a hundred instruments of torture. Distant bells were tolling mournfully. A priest advanced holding aloft a crucifix and chanting in sepulchral voice:

"The hour of heretics sounds."

Louder and funereally rang the dismal bells; the torturers drew near; I struggled to rise to my feet — and awoke.

The bells of the monastery were booming out over the night.

CHAPTER XI

CRUMBLING CITIES

IT was well along in the next afternoon that I descended at the station of Ávila and climbed a long dusty mile into the city. A scent of the dim, half-forgotten past hovered over the close-walled, peculiarly garbed place. When I had made a circuit of her ancient wall, through which her no less time-worn cathedral thrusts its hips, I drifted down into the dusty vega below, where in the church of Santo Tomás sleeps the dead hope of "los reyes católicos." If the sculptor be trustworthy the prince would have been an intelligent, kindly lad, even though his martial valor might never have rivaled that of his stout-hearted mother. Returned to the city, I strolled for an hour along the lofty Paséo del Rastro, watching the sun sink red behind the serrated jumble of mountains on the far western horizon, beyond which lay my next stopping-place; and so to bed in the Posada de la Estrella amid the munching asses and snoring arrieros.

Ávila is connected with Salamanca by rail, but the route forms a sharp angle with its apex many miles

to the north. I had decided, therefore, to walk.
Swinging down through the western city gate and
across the babbling Adaja by the aged stone
bridge, I clambered again upward to where a huge
stone cross invites to a rest in its shade and a final
retrospect of crumbling Avila and her many-tur-
reted, constraining wall. An easy two-days' walk
lay before me. For had not Herr Baedeker, so
seldom in error as to plain facts, announced the
distance as thirty-five miles?

As I wended on up the hillside, however, I was
suddenly stricken profane by a stone sign-post
rising before me with the dismal greeting:

" Salamanca 99 kilómetros."

Herr Baedeker was wrong by a little matter of
thirty miles.

But I had set the time of my entrance into
Salamanca; delay would bring havoc to my delicately
adjusted itinerary. I doubled my pace.

The way led through a country as savage of
aspect as any in Spain, waterless, dusty, glaring,
overspread with huge rocks tumbled pell-mell as if
the Mason of the universe had thrown here the
materials left over from His building. By afternoon a few lean farms began to crowd their way
in between the rocks, now and then a sturdy, thick-
set tree found place, and over all nature hovered
great clouds of locusts whose refrain reminded how

euphonious is the Spaniard's name for what we dub
"dog days,"—"canta la chicharra—the locust
sings." The inhabitants of the region seemed
somewhat more in fortune's favor than the rest
of the peninsula. Passing peasants, though rare,
had none a hungry look; their carts were fancifully carved and painted both on body and wheels,
while the trappings of their cattle were decorative
in the extreme.

All a summer day I tramped forward over hill
and hollow toward the great jagged range, the
hardy trees dying out, the fields growing in size and
number, but the sierra seeming to hold ever as far
aloof. Beyond a small withered forest in which
were roaming flocks of brown goats, I climbed a
steady five miles to a summit village exhibiting every
outward sign of poverty and most fittingly named
"Salvadios—God save us." The keeper of its
one quasi-public house deigned after long argu-
ment to set before me a lame excuse for supper, but
loudly declined to furnish lodging. I withdrew,
therefore, to a threshing-floor across the way,
heaped high with still unbroken bundles of wheat,
and put in a shiveringly cold night—so great is
the contrast between the seething plains by day and
this hilltop bitten by every wind—not once falling
into a sound sleep for the gaunt, savage curs that
prowled about me.

At dawn I was already afoot and three hours

later entered the city of Peñaranda, in the outskirts of which a fine plaza de toros was building,
but within all the confines of which was no evidence
of school, library, nor indeed of restaurant. I
contented myself with a bit of fruit and trudged on.
This may not, perhaps, have been the hottest day
of all that Spanish summer, but it bore certainly all
the earmarks thereof. The earth lay cracked and
blistered about me, the trees writhing with the heat,
the rays rising from the rocky soil like a dense
stage-curtain of steam. In a shriveled and parched
pueblo of mud huts, exactly resembling the villages
of Palestine, I routed out a kindly old woman for
a foreshortened lunch; and then on again in the
inferno, choking fields of grain and vineyards soon
becoming numerous on either hand. The wise
husbandmen, however, had sought refuge, and in all
the grilling landscape was not a human being to
be seen, save and except a sweat-dripping pedestrian from foreign parts straining along the
scorching highway.

This swung at length to the right, swooped
down through a river that had not a drop of water,
and staggering to the top of an abrupt knoll,
showed me far off, yet in all distinctness, a rich
reddish-brown city gathered together on a low hilltop and terminating in glinting spires. It was
Salamanca; and of all the cities I have come thus
upon unheralded and from the unpeopled highway

none can rival her in richness of color, like ripe old
wine, a city that has grown old gracefully and with
increasing beauty. So fascinating the sight that
I sat down beneath the solitary tree by the way to
gaze upon it — and to swing half round the circuit
of the shrub as the sun drove the scanty shadow
before it.

But I was still far off the golden-brown city and,
setting slowly onward in the descending evening, I
all but encircled the place before the carretera,
coming upon the ancient puente romano, clambered
upward into its unrivaled Plaza Mayor.

Just back of this, four stories above the Plaza
de la Verduga, or Place of the Green Stuff, lives
a widow whose little spare chamber is let in the
winter season to some unpretentious student of the
now unpretentious university. I engaged this,
together with what of physical nourishment should
be reasonable, at three pesetas a day. As I took
possession, the daughter of the hostess, a muchacha
of eight, peered in upon me hugging a doll under
one arm.

"Qué muñeca más bonita!" I hazarded, which
turned out to be unwise, for the homage so overcame her diffidence that she came in not only to
offer the information that my complexion strangely
resembled that of a lobster in the salmantino
museum, but such a fund of further information that
it was long before I had inveigled her outside the

door and, throwing myself on the bed, slept the clock round.

As in many another city it had been my fortune to reach Salamanca on the eve of one of her great ·festivals. Indeed, that must be a foresighted traveler who can journey through Spain without being frequently caught up in the whirlpool of some local fiesta. The excuse this time was Assumption Day. The festivities within the city walls offered nothing of extraordinary, being chiefly confined to a band concert in the central plaza. Richer by far would be the richest city of the earth could she purchase and transplant into her own midst the Plaza Mayor of Salamanca, with its small forest of palms, the rich brown medallioned façades and surrounding colonnades beneath which the salmantino is wont to stroll, la salmantina on his arm, while the band plays in the flower-shrouded stand in its center. Salamanca might sell, too, in spite of her boast that it is the finest in Spain, being poorer than the proverbial church mouse, were she not also Spanish and prouder than she is poor.

The real fiesta, however, took the form of a bullfight that had a character all its own. Salamanca, as I have hinted, is no longer a city of wealth. Indeed, those occasions are rare in these modern days when she can indulge in a round of the national sport, even though she possesses one of the largest bullrings in Spain. On this great

holiday, however, the city fathers had decided that
nothing within the bounds of reason was too good
for the recreating of Salamanca's long unfeasted
children. A full-sized bullfight would, to be sure,
have far overstepped the bounds above mentioned.
But after long debate and deep investigation it had
been concluded that a córrida with four bulls, no
horses, one real matador, and seats of all shades and
distinctions at one peseta each might be conceded.

With this unlimited choice of vantage-points at
my own price I went out early to the plaza and
picked my place in the sombra in what was evidently
a section reserved for the guardia civil; for before
long the guards, in full uniform and their three-
cornered hats, began to gather about me, first in
pairs, then in groups, then in swarms, until I was
wholly shut in and surrounded by guardias civiles
like a dandelion in the center of a bed of tulips.
Far from resenting my intrusion, however, if such
it was, they initiated me into their order with botas
and cigarettes and included me in their conversation and merriment during the rest of the day.

The entertainment began at four. With that exception, however, it had few points of similarity
with the regulation córrida. The procession entered, fully six men in torero garb — though that
of two or three of them fitted like amateur theatrical
costumes — followed by two horsemen, two, in
their shirt-sleeves, as was also señor el alcalde in

One of the Bombita family

Machaquito—Spain's greatest bull-fighter

"Aficionados del sol"

Peasants in Sunday best

his box. The key thrown, the fight began; with the elimination of the one unquestionably unpleasant feature,— the killing of horses. Even aged hacks cost money and, as I have already more than once suggested, money is a rare commodity in Salamanca. When the bull had been worried a bit with the cloaks, the banderilleros proceeded at once to plant their darts. The professional matador, a young man rejoicing in the name of Trueno — " Thunder "— had, therefore, a far more difficult task than usual, for more than anything else it is the venting of his rage and strength on the blindfolded steeds that tires the bull, and on this occasion it was a still wild and comparatively fresh animal which the diestro was called upon to face. He despatched his three allotted bulls, however, without accident and to the vociferous satisfaction of the audience, which filled even at the low price only a bit more than the shaded section. It was not, as the guardia beside me was at some pains to explain, that there were not salmantinos quite sufficient to pack the plaza to overflowing, but that there were not pesetas enough in town to go round. In the throng, too, were no small number of peasants from all the widely surrounding country, some in the old dress with knee breeches.

But to touch upon the unusual features of the córrida. As a part of the worrying of the second bull a chulo placed a chair in the ring and, stand-

ing upon it with neither weapon nor cloak, awaited
the charge.   When the bull had all but reached him
he sprang suddenly into the air, the animal dashed
under him and, falling upon the unoffending article
of furniture, dissolved it thoroughly into its com-
ponent parts and scattered them broadcast about the
arena.

The most nerve-thrilling performance, however,
that it was my privilege to see in all the devil-may-
care land of Spain was the feat that followed immediately on the death of the chair-wrecker.   It
was the " star attraction " of the day and was announced on the posters in all the Spaniard's richness
of superlatives — and he is a born and instinctive
writer of " ads."   Clinging as closely as possible to
the eloquent phraseology of the original the announcement may be set forth in near-English as
follows:

" Various are the chances (tricks) which are
executed in the different plazas of Spain inside
the taurine art, but none that has more called attention than that which is practised by José
Villar son of the memorable matador (killer,
murderer) of bulls Villarillo who "— not father
Illo, who has left off all earthly sport, but son José
—" locating himself in the center of the arena and
placed with the head towards below and the feet by
above imploring the public to maintain the most impressive silence during the risk (fate) consummates

'the trick (chance) of Tancredo; very well, this
Management not reflecting on (sparing) either expense or sacrifice has contracted with him in order
that he shall fulfill (lift, pull off; *sic.*) this trick
(risk) on the third bull to the end that the salmantinos shall know it, with which program this Management believes to have filled to the full the desires of
the aficionados (rooters, fans, amateurs)."

The second bull, therefore, having been ignomini-
ously dragged to oblivion and the butcher-shop, and
the blood patches of the arena resanded, there sallied
forth from the further gate a small, athletic man
of thirty-five or so, hatless — and partly hairless —
dressed from head to foot in the brightest red, of a
material so thin that the movement of his every
muscle could be plainly seen beneath it. He was entirely empty-handed. He marched with sprightly
stride across the ring and, bowing low to the alcalde
in his box above, addressed to the public a warning
and an entreaty to maintain the utmost silence during
the " consummation of the risk." An assistant then
appeared, carrying a small wooden box with a piece of
gas-pipe six feet long fixed upright in the top of it.
This Villar placed exactly in the center of the ring,
a hundred yards or more in every direction from the
barrier. Across the gas-pipe, near the top, he
fastened a much shorter piece, thus forming a cross.
On the box he placed a circular roll of cloth, stood on
his head thereon, hooked his toes over the cross-piece,

waved a hand gaily to the public, and folded his arms. Every other torero stepped outside the ring, and the toril gate swung open.

A wild snort, and there plunged into the arena as powerful and savage a brute as it had ever yet been my lot to see. For an instant he stood motionless, blinking in the blinding sunlight. Then suddenly catching sight of the statue flaming with the hated color, he shot away toward it with the speed of an express-train — a Spanish express at least — until, a bare three feet from it, he stopped instantly stone-still by thrusting out his forelegs like a Western broncho, then slowly, gingerly tiptoed up to the motionless figure, sniffed at it, and turned and trotted away.

The public burst forth in a thunderclap of applause. Villar got right end up as calmly and gracefully as a French count in a drawing-room, laid a hand on his heart, and smiling serenely, bowed once, twice, th —— and just then a startled roar went up from the tribunes, for the bull had suddenly turned and, espying the man in red, dashed at him with lowered horns and a bellow of anger.

There is nowhere registered, so far as my investigations carry, the record of José Villar, son of Villarillo, in the hundred-yard dash. But this much may be asserted with all assurance, that it has in it nothing of that slow, languid, snail-like pace of the ten-second college champion. Which was well; for

"Aficionados del sol"

Peasants in Sunday best

some two inches below his flying heels, as he set a new record likewise in the vaulting of barriers, the murderous horns crashed into the oak plank tablas with the sound of a freight collision and an earnestness that gave work to the plaza carpenters for some twenty minutes to come.

Therein Villar was more fortunate than the Mexican Tancredo, inventor of the " suerte," and for whom it was named. Tancredo, like Dr. Guillotin, was overreached by his own invention, for while his record for the hundred was but a second or two less than that of Villar, it was just this paltry margin that made him, on the day next following his last professional appearance, the chief though passive actor in a spectacle of quite a different character.

The " Suerte de Tancredo " has never won any vast amount of popularity in Spain, except with the spectators. Toreros in general manifest a hesitation akin to bashfulness in thus seeking the plaudits of the multitude. By reason of which diffidence among his fellows, José, son of Villarillo, memorable matador de toros, pockets after each such recreation a sum that might not seem overwhelming to an American captain of industry or to a world-famous tenor, but one which the average Spaniard cannot name in a single breath.

Salamanca's day of amusement did not, however, by any means end here. Beneath the name of " Thunder," the professional matador, there was
14

printed with equal bombast that of FERNANDO
MARTÍN. Now Fernando was quite evidently a
salmantino butt, a tall gawky fellow whose place in
the society of Salamanca was apparently very simi-
liar to that of those would-be or has-been baseball
players to be found vegetating in many of our
smaller towns. Like them, too, Fernando was in all
probability wont to hover about the pool-rooms and
dispensing-parlors of his native city, boasting of his
untested prowess at the national game. That his
talents might not, therefore, forever remain hidden
under a wineglass, and also, perhaps, because his services might be engaged at five hundred pesetas less
than the five hundred that a professional sobresaliente
would have demanded, the thoughtful city fathers had
caused him to be set down on the program, likewise in striking type, as " SUBSTITUTE WITH NE-
CESSITY (CON NECESIDAD) TO KILL THE FOURTH
BULL."

It was this " necesidad " that worked the undoing
of Fernando Martín. When the customary by-play
had been practised on the fourth animal, enter Fernando with bright red muleta, false pigtail, glinting
sword, and anything but the sure-of-one's-self countenance of a professional espada. He faced the
brute first directly in front of the block of guardias
civiles, and the nearest he came to laying the animal
low at the first thrust was to impale on a horn and
sadly mutilate a sleeve of his own gay and rented

jacket. The crowd jeered, as crowds will the world over at the sight of a man whose father and mother and even grandfather they have known for years trying to prove himself the equal of men imported from elsewhere. Fernando advanced again, manœuvering for position, though with a peculiar movement of the knees not usual among toreros, and which was all too visible to every eye in the hooting multitude. Trueno, the professional, stuck close at his side in spite of the clamorous demand of the public that he leave the salmantino to play out his own game unhampered. Martín hazarded two or three more nerveless thrusts, with no other damage, thanks to the watchful eye and cloak of Trueno, than one toss of ten feet and a bleeding groin. By this time the jeering of his fellow-townsmen had so overshadowed the tyro's modicum of good sense that he turned savagely on his protector and ordered him to leave the ring. Fortunately Trueno was not of the stuff to take umbrage at the insults of a foolish man in a rage, or the population of Salamanca would incontestably have been reduced by one before that merry day was done.

The utmost length of time between the entrance of a professional matador for the last act and the death of the bull is four or five minutes. Fernando Martín trembled and toiled away ten, twenty, thirty, forty. Slowly, but certainly and visibly his bit of courage oozed away; the peculiar movement of his

knees grew more and more pronounced. No longer
daring to meet the bull face to face, he skulked along
the barrier until the animal's tail was turned and,
dashing past him at full speed, stabbed backward
at his neck as he ran, to the uproarious merriment
of the spectators. Trueno saved his life certainly
a score of times. At last, when the farce had run
close upon fifty minutes, a signal from the alcalde
sent across the arena the sharp note of a bugle, two
cabestros, or trained steers were turned into the ring,
and the bull, losing at once all belligerency, trotted
docilely away with them. The star of Fernando
Martín, would-be matador de toros, was forever set,
and if he be not all immune to ridicule his native
city surely knows him no more.

It is law that no bull that has once entered the
ring shall live. Curious to know what was to be the
fate of this animal, I sprang over the barrier and
hurried across to the gate by which he had disappeared. There I beheld a scene that forever dispelled any notion that the task of the matador is an
easy one, however simple it may look from the tribunes. The bull was threshing to and fro within a
small corral, bellowing with rage and lashing the air
with his tail. It required six men and a half-hour of
time to lasso and drag him to the fence. With a
hundred straining at the rope his head was drawn
down under the gate, a man struck him several blows
with a sledge, and another, watching his opportunity,

swung his great navaja and laid wide open the animal's throat.

It was late when, having mingled for some time with the country folk dancing on the sandy plain before the plaza, I returned to the city for my bundle and repaired to the station. A twelve-hour ride was before me. For I had decided to explore a territory where even the scent of tourists is unknown,— the northwest province of Galicia.

The train that I boarded at eleven was crowded with countrymen returning from the day's festival, a merry but in no sense intoxicated company, in which I saw my first wooden-shod Galicians. The car was, for once, of the American pattern — though of Spanish width — with thirty seats each large enough for three persons. The brakeman, too, who stood lantern on arm in the open door, bore an unusual resemblance to an American " shack."

A dozen men were standing in the aisle, but to my surprise one seat near the center of the car seemed to be unoccupied. When I reached it, however, I found a priest stretched out on his back, his hands clasped over his paunch, snoring impressively. I carried a protest to the brakeman and with a snort he swooped down upon the sleeper. At sight of him, however, he recoiled.

" Carajo! " he cried. " Es un padre! I could n't disturb his reverence."

I stooped and touched the monopolist on the shoulder, being in no mood to remain standing all night. Moreover, I had long been curious to know the Spaniard's attitude toward a man who should treat a priest as an ordinary human being. "His reverence" grunted. I touched him again. His snore lost a beat or two and began once more. I shook him more forcibly. He opened his blood-shot eyes, snorted "Huh!" so much like a certain monopolist of the animal kingdom that even the passengers about me laughed at the resemblance — and fell again to snoring. I sat down gently on his fat legs and, when he kicked me off, confiscated a place. He sat up with the look of a man whose known world has suddenly crumbled about his ears and glared at me with bulging eyes a full two minutes, while over the faces of the onlookers flitted a series of winks and smiles.

He was just huddling himself up again in the two-thirds of the seat that remained to him when the door opened and Trueno, the matador, his little *coleta* peeping out from beneath his hat, his sword-case under one arm, entered and, spying the extra place, sat down in it with scant ceremony. We fell to talking. The torero was a jovial, explosive, devil-may-care fellow who looked and dressed his character well. The priest slunk off somewhere in the thickest hours and his place was taken by a peasant who had been standing near me since leaving Salamanca.

When he found opportunity to break into the conversation he addressed me with an amused smile:

" You are not then a Catholic, señor? "

" No."

" Ah! A socialist! " he cried with assurance.

For to the masses of southern Europe socialist and non-Catholic are synonymous.

" I doubt, señor," I observed, " whether you yourself are a Catholic."

" Cómo, señor! " he cried, raising his hands in a comical gesture of quasi-horror. " I, a cristino viejo, no Catholic! "

" Do you go to church and do what your cura commands? "

" What nonsense! " he cried, using a still more forcible term. " Who does? My wife goes now and then to confession. I go to church, señor, to be baptized, married, and buried."

" Why go then? "

" Caramba! " he gasped. " How else shall a man be buried, married, and baptized? "

Toward morning I fell into a doze, from which I was awakened by the extraordinary sensation of feeling cold. Dawn was touching the far horizon. The train was straining upward through a sharply rising country. As the sun rose we came in sight of Astorga, standing drearily on her bleak hilltop, and in memory of Gil Blas and for the unlimbering of my legs I alighted and climbed into the town. It proved

as uninteresting as any in Spain, and before the morn
ing was old I was again riding northwestward.
Soon there came an utter change of scene; tunnels
grew unaccountable, the railroad winding its way
doggedly upward through a wild, heavily wooded
mountain region that had little in common with familiar Spanish landscapes. In mid-afternoon I dis-
mounted at the station of Lugo, the capital of
Galicia.

CHAPTER XII

WILDEST SPAIN

NEAREST of all the Iberian peninsula to our own land, the ancient kingdom of Galicia is as well-nigh unknown to us as any section of Europe. As far back as mankind's memory carries it has been Spain's "last ditch." Up into this wild mountain corner of the peninsula retreated in its turn each subdued race as conqueror after conqueror swept over the land,— the aboriginal Iberians before the Celts, the Celtiberians before the coast-hugging Phœnicians and Carthaginians, these before the omniverous Romans, followed as the centuries rolled on by Vandal, Suevi, Goth and Moor. Further they could not flee, for behind them the world falls away by sheer cragged cliffs into the fathomless sea. Here the fugitives melted together into a racial amalgam, an uncourageous amalgam on the whole, for in each case those who reached the fastnesses were that remnant of the race that preferred life to honor, those who "fought and ran away," or who took to their heels even earlier in the proceedings.

Yet it was a long two centuries after Hannibal had followed his father Hasdrubal into the Stygian realms of the defeated, after Rome had covered the rest of the peninsula with that network of roads that remains to this day, that the power of the outside world pushed its way into this tumbled wilderness. But for the necessity of loot to pay the gambling debts of his merry youth the conqueror indeed might never have appeared. Yet appear he did, — a young Roman just beginning to display a crownal baldness, known to his legions as Cæsar and answering to his friends of the Roman boulevards and casinos to the name of Julius. He conquered; and when he, too, had written his memoirs and passed his perforated way, that lucky heir of all Roman striving caused to be built in these his mountains a city that should — like all that sprouted or grew under his reign — bear his name,—"Lucus Augusti — Gus's place."

To-day it is Lugo, a modest city ensconced in the lap of a plain near a thousand feet above the railway station that bears its name. Politically Spanish, it is so in little else. The last traces of the Arab, so indelible in the rest of the peninsula, have disappeared. The racial amalgam, now the *gallego*, is close akin to the Portuguese, like all long dominated peoples docile, unassertive, born to be a servant to mankind. He is the chief butt, the low comedian of the Spanish stage, slow, loutish, heavy of mind and body, without a suggestion of the fire of that bubbling child of enthusiasm, the Andaluz; none of the native dignity and consciousness of personal worth of the Castilian, not even the dreaminess of the Manchegan. He is fitted to be what he is,— the domestic, the server of his fellow-countrymen.

From the posada at the city gate I climbed to Lugo's chief promenade and Alameda, the top of her surrounding wall. This is some forty feet high, of flat, irregular slabs of slate-stone on Roman foundations, with a circuit of nearly a mile and a half. The town within and below is of the same material, the dull gray or drab so predominating as to give the place the somberness of a stone village of Wales. The inhabitants, moreover, have little of the Spaniard's love of color, being as sober in garb as in demeanor. It is noteworthy that those communities that are least embellished by nature are most prone to garb themselves in all the colors of the spectrum. The Venetian above his muddy water has been noted in all times as a colorist; the peasants of the Apennines barely a hundred miles away have very little brightness of dress.

So the Lugense; for if the town itself is somber gray, the moss and vines that overrun the low, leaden houses, the gardens scattered among them, the flowers that trail from the windows of the dwellings built medieval-fashion into the walls make the scene gay even within. While outwardly it in unsurpassed. From the wall-top promenade the eye commands an endless vista of richest green landscape, a labyrinth of munificent hill forms and mountain ridges dense-wooded with veritable Alpine forests rolling away on every side to the uttermost horizon.

In the town itself is almost nothing of what the tourist calls " sights "; which is, perhaps, a chief reason why his shadow almost never falls within it. There is only the dull, bluish-stone cathedral, and an atmosphere wholly individual; nothing exciting, nothing extraordinary, though one amusing detail of life is sure to attract attention. Like many towns of Spain, Lugo obtains her water through the mouths of stone lions in her central plaza. But here the fountain spouts are for some Gallegan reason high above the flagging, far out of reach. Whence the plaza and the streets of the city are at all hours overrun with housewives and domestics carrying not merely pitchers but a tin tube some ten feet long through which to conduct the water into their receptacles. In nothing does the town differ from familiar Spain more than in temperature. Her climate is like that of Bar Harbor. A change in a few hours as from Florida in August to Mount Desert brought quickly home to me the fact that my garb was fitted only for perpetual summer. Almost with the setting sun I fell visibly to shivering, and by dark I was forced to take refuge in bed.

I had come into Galicia proposing to strike across

country to Oviedo, capital of the Asturias, in the hope of getting wholly and thoroughly "off the beaten track." Therein I seemed fully to have succeeded. Inquiries in Lugo elicited the information that Oviedo was reputed to lie somewhere to the eastward. Nothing more; except some nebulous notion of a highway beginning at the base of the city wall leading for a day or two in that direction. For which uncertainty I was in no sense sorry, delighted with the prospect of exploring by a route of my own that wooded wilderness of mountains that spreads endlessly away from Lugo's promenade, certain of finding a land and a people unsullied by tourists.

Dinner over on the day after my arrival, I descended from the city of Augustus by the unpaved road that was to set me a little way on my journey. It was soon burrowing through dense, scented forests, broken by scores of little deep green meadows along the way; so many and so inviting that it required a strong tug of the will to keep from lying down for a nap in each of them, in memory of the many grassless, siestaless, fly-bitten days in the rest of the peninsula. Truly the good things of this world are unevenly distributed. In fact, only by a dead lift of the imagination could one comprehend that this also was Spain. Switzerland, perhaps, but never a part and portion of the same country with the sear, deforested uplands of Castille, the

sandy stretches of Andalusia, with osseous and all
but treeless La Mancha. The division line between
Europe and Africa was meant surely to be the
Pyrenees and this Cantabrian range rather than the
Mediterranean.

When darkness settled down I halted at a jumbled
stone hamlet, where payment was refused except for
the few cents' worth of peasant fare I ate. For my
bed, was spread in an open stable a bundle of newly
threshed wheat-straw that was longer than myself.
A half-day's tramp had not left me sleepy. The
night lay cool and silent about me, and I sank into
that reverie of contentment that comes most surely
upon the wanderer when he has left the traveled
world behind and turns his face care-free toward the
unknown, that mysterious land across which beck-
ons the aërial little sprite men name *Wanderlust*.
For the joy of travel is not in arriving but in setting
forth, in moving onward; how fast matters little,
where, even less, but ever on and on, forgetting, for
the supremest satisfaction, that there is a goal to
attain. Let a man wander away into unknown lands
smiling with summer, his journey's end little more
than conjecture, his day of arrival a matter of indifference, and if he feel not then the joy of the
open road he may know for a certainty that he is
a hug-the-hearth, and no gipsy and a vagabond.

In the morning continued a roadway hobble-
skirted by forests, a country as pleasing as Caruso's

voice, as soothing to the traveler from stony Spain as McDowell's music. To enumerate the details of life and landscape here is merely to tell by contrast what the rest of Spain is not. The inhabitants were in the highest degree laconic, as taciturn as the central and southern Spaniard is garrulous, self-conscious to the point of bashfulness, a characteristic as uncommon in the rest of the country as among the Jews or Arabs; a heavy-handed, unobserving peasantry that passed the stranger unaccosted, almost unnoticed. Such conversation as exchanged must be introduced by the traveler. The cheering "Vaya!" was heard no more, the stock greeting being a mumbled "Buenos."

In appearance, be the inspection not too close, this mountain people well deserves the outworn epithet "picturesque." The women young and old wore on their heads large kerchiefs of brilliant red, and most of them a waist of the same color, offering striking contrast to the rich green background, as the latter was sure to be. As footwear, except those unpossessed of any, both sexes had wooden shoes painted black and fancifully carved, which, scraping along the highway, carried the thoughts quickly back to Japan. At nearer sight, however, something of the picturesqueness was lost in the unfailing evidences of a general avoidance of the bath and washtub.

Of least interest were the dwellings of this peas-

antry,— villages neither frequent nor large, more
properly mere heaps of gray huts built without
order or plan of the slate-stone of which the province itself is chiefly formed, as was seen wherever
the outer soil had been stripped away and the skele-
ton of the mountain laid bare. For all the character of the country abundance of rain and a pains-
taking agriculture gave good crops. Galicia indeed
supports, though in poverty, the densest population
of the peninsula. Wheat, Indian corn, and hay
abounded. The former was stacked, and threshed
with flails — two customs unknown in Spain, as the
latter products are entirely. The maize was sown.
A species of cabbage on a stalk some two feet long
was among the most common of the vegetables.

All these products grew, not on the level, but in
little isolated, precipitous fields in which it seemed
impossible that the laborers, male and female with
sickles or mattocks, could stand upright. Flocks of
sheep and goats were many, and as the final change
from the Spain that I had hitherto known there was
nowhere silence. The forests on either hand were
vocal with the songs of birds. Mountain streams
came plunging headlong down the ravines, or
brawled along through stony channels beside the
winding way. The water was of the purest and
clearest, which may, perhaps, have led the inhabitants to give most of their mundifying attention to
the vessels in which it was carried,— great oaken

buckets each with three wide hoops scoured spotless and shining as a Hindu's *lota*.

But most unfailing breakers of the silence and most characteristic of all the features of the province was its vehicles. The Phrygian peasants who dragged their produce into Troy before the siege had certainly as up-to-date a conveyance. The traveler's first encounter with one of these Homeric contrivances is sure to be startling. There is only one word that exactly expresses their sound from afar, — the French *bourdonner* — the noise of the bumblebee. Indeed, when first I heard it I fell to threshing about my ears, sure that one of those insects was upon me. Slowly the sound grew to the meowling of a thousand cats, and around a turn of the forest-hedged road came a peasant's cart drawn by little brown oxen — they are as often cows — much like our Jerseys in appearance, a great sheepskin thrown over their heads, to the horns of which the yoke was fastened. The unwieldy edifice, wabbling drunkenly as it came, consisted of little more than two solid disks of wood like cistern covers turning on a wooden axle, the whole having about it neither an ounce of iron nor a smell of axle-grease. Its pace certainly did not exceed a mile an hour, the oxen see-sawing from side to side of the road, twisting their burdened heads to stare at me with curious, sad eyes. As it passed, my ears literally ached with its scream. I doubled my pace to flee the

15

torture. But there was no entire escape; hardly once thereafter was I out of sound of a cart or two, now screaming by, now " bourdonning " away across some valley, buzzing at times even after the night had settled down.

Early on this second day, which was Sunday, there appeared a far more precipitous and rocky country through which the road began to wind its way upward amid a chaos of rugged tumbled valleys, gaining by early afternoon an elevation above the line of vegetation. For two hours I kept lookout for a bit of level space for a siesta, without finding a patch of flat ground as large as my knapsack. I stepped over the edge of the highway and lay down on a bank so sheer that I was obliged to brace my stick against the small of my back to keep from pitching down the thousand-foot slope into a brook; and even as it was I awoke to find I had shifted some ten feet down the hill.

The ascent thereafter grew still sharper, the surrounding world being at last wholly enveloped in a dense cloud. From out of this I heard, at what I fancied must be toward sunset, sounds of revelry, by which, marching onward, I was soon encompassed, though still unseeing and unseen. Suddenly there came waltzing toward me out of the fog a couple in each other's arms, disappearing again as another pair whirled forth out of the unknown. Wandering on through a merry but invisible multitude I ran all but into the arms of two guardias civiles leaning on their muskets. They greeted me with vast surprise, welcoming me to their mountain-top town of Fonsagrada and, far from demanding my papers, offered to find me a partner that I might join the village in its Sunday celebration on the green. I declined such hilarity, but for an hour stood chatting with them while the dancers whirled unseen about us.

Fonsagrada has no regular accommodations for strangers. The peregrinating band of musicians, however, furnishing the day's melody, was to be cared for in a sort of grocery, to which I repaired with them when the dance was over. Having partaken of a substantial supper in which the far-famed *bacalao* — cod preserved in great chunks in barrels like salt pork; a main staple in this region — made its initial appearance, I laid my case before the proprietor. He was a Yankee-like man in the middle thirties, of modern business methods even though he knew next to nothing of the world outside his cloud-bound village. Notwithstanding, therefore, that there was no " costumbre " to sanction it, he bade me spend the night under his roof — which I did all too literally, for when I had left off swapping yarns with the melodious nomads my host led the way to the garret, half-filled with straw, where in the midst of a too realistic dream I rose up suddenly and all but shattered my head on the roof in question.

In the morning the clouds were still wandering like

lost souls through the streets of Fonsagrada. A
mist that barely escaped being a rain was falling
when I set off in an attempt to follow the voluminous
directions of the dubious village. According to these,
when I had passed the " Mesón de Galo," a lonely
stone tavern a few miles out, I left the road, which
was bending toward Gijón on the north coast, and
fell into a descending mountain path. A tang of the
salt sea was in the air. All the day through I
climbed, slipped, and scrambled over jagged mountain
slopes and through deep, rocky barrancas. There
develops with much wandering an instinct to follow
the right fork of a mountain trail, slight hints that
could not be explained, but without the half-uncon-
scious noting of which I must have gone a score of
times astray. Twice or thrice I stumbled into a hamlet in some wrinkle of the range, a village of five or
six hovels huddling in the shadow of an enormous,
overtowering church, all built of flat field stones and
swarming with huge white dogs.

At Grandas, a bit larger village overhung by
massed up mountains, I was at length so fortunate
as to get after much search an intangible imitation
of a meal. From there I panted a long time upward
and came out at last above a seemingly bottomless
gorge, a gorge so deep that I had scrambled nearly
a half-hour along its brink before I noted that far
down in its depths was a town, encircled by vertical
vineyards, like embroidery on the lower skirts of its

overhanging mountains. My path lay plainly visible
on the opposite slope, only a long jump away, but a
jump for Pegasus or the princess of the Rosstrappe,
and I, mere mortal, was forced to wind a long hour
and a half to and fro on the rubbled face of the
mountain before I entered the town below, called
Saline.

Before me lay the most laborious task of all my
Spanish journey. A mountain as nearly perpendicular as man could hope to ascend, without a break
or a knoll in all its slope, rose, a sheer wall, certainly
four thousand feet above. The gorge seemed some
boundary set by the gods between two worlds. Up
the face of the cliff a path had been laid out with
mathematical precision, every one of its score of legs
a toilsome climb over loose stones, with the sun, un-
tempered by a breath of wind, pouring down its fury
upon my back. It was hot as Spain in the depth of
the canyon; it was chilling cold when I reached the
summit heavily crested in clouds and threw myself
down breathless on my back. Darkness was coming
on, and I fell soon to shivering in the biting mountain
air and must rise and hurry forward. It was not
strange that in the fog and darkness instinct failed
and that when finally I reached a village of eight or
nine hovels and inquired its name the inhabitants replied " Figuerina," not in the least like the " La
Mesa " I had expected.

Of a brawny, weather-beaten girl milking a cow

by the light of a torch in what passed for the principal street, I asked:

"Is there a posada in town?"

"No sé, señor," she answered.

"Don't know! When your town has only nine houses?"

But she only stared dully at me through the gloom, and I carried my inquiry elsewhere. With no better result, however, for each one I asked returned the same laconic, "I don't know." I had sat down on a boulder in the center of the hamlet to puzzle over this strange ignorance when a strapping mountaineer approached through the darkness and led me with few words to the house of the head man. The latter was in bed with a broken leg, having had the misfortune to fall off his farm a few days before. I was taken before him as he lay propped up with pillows and, after a few brief questions, he commanded his family to make me at home.

Only at a distance are these mountain hamlets of northern Spain inviting. For the good people live, indoors and out, in peace and equality with their pigs and chickens, not because they are by nature unclean, but because they know no other life than this, nor any reason why their domestic animals should not be treated as equals. The wife of the village chief led me into the living-room and kitchen. I knew it was that, for she said so. The place was absolutely dark. Since leaving Lugo I had not seen a pane of glass, and lamps of any sort appear to be unknown in these hamlets of the Sierra de Rañadoiro. There was, to be sure, a bit of fire in one corner, but it gave not the slighest illumination, only a thick smoke that wandered about looking for an exit, and unsuccessfully, for there was nothing whatever in the way of chimney, and the door had been closed as we entered. Smoker though I am, I began to weep and did not once leave off while I remained in the room.

The mustiness of a dungeon assailed the nostrils; the silence was broken by a continual droning. The floor was stone. In the room were six or eight men and women, as I discovered little by little from their voices. Supper was announced, and a match I struck showed an indistinct group of which I was a part humped over a steaming kettle in the center of the floor. Into this all began to dip their bread. I hung back, which the wife discovering by some instinct, she made an exclamation I did not understand and soon after there was thrust into my hands a private bowl of the concoction.

It turned out to be a " caldo gallego "— an all but tasteless thick soup of which the chief ingredient, besides water, is the long-stemmed cabbage indigenous to the region. A spoon was then handed me. It was of wood, homemade, and flat as a canoe-paddle. What most aroused my wonder was the bread. A glimpse I had caught of it in the flicker of my

match seemed to show a loaf of about the size of a
large grindstone — though I charged this to optical
illusion — from which wedges were cut, one of them
being laid in my lap. It was coarse as mortar, yet
as savory, and proved later to be as sustaining a
bread as I have yet run across on the earth. This
and the caldo being no match for a mountain-climbing
appetite, I asked the privilege of buying a bowl of
milk. From my unseen companions arose many
ejaculations of wonder that I could afford such a
luxury, but a bowl of it was soon put in my hands.
A better milk I never broke bread in.

Still I was at a loss to account for the incessant
droning in the room, like the croak of a distant ox-
cart. Since my entrance, too, I had been struck a
thousand times lightly in the face, as with bread
crumbs or the paper-wads indigenous to the old
country schoolhouse. When it occurred to me to put
the two mysteries together both were solved. The
flies were so thick in the room that they made this
sound in flying blindly back and forth.

But once upstairs the dwelling assumed a new
rating. Here was, it is true, no luxury; but the
rough-fashioned chamber, partly store-room and
partly spare bedroom, was capacious and clean, of
the rough, unused sort of cleanliness of a farmer's
" best room," opened only on extraordinary occasions. The one sheet of the massive bed was as stiff
as any windjammer's mainsail, the blanket as rough

as the robe of a Cistercian monk. Among a score of multiform articles stored in the room was a stack of bread such as I had eaten below, some forty loaves each fully as large as a half-bushel measure. It is baked from four to six months ahead, twice or thrice a year, and has a crust hard and impervious as a glazed pot, which keeps it fresh and savory for an almost unlimited period.

As I bade farewell to my host next morning I held out to him two pesetas. He resented the offer as an Arab or a Castilian might have, but being of those accustomed to express themselves less in words than in actions, did so laconically. When I offered it again he rose half up on his elbows and bellowed "No!" His gruffness was in no sense from anger, but merely his mode of speaking emphatically, and a way of hiding that bashfulness so common to mountaineers, who are usually, as here, a shy and kindly people with much more genuine benevolence than grace of manner. I protested that I should at least be permitted to pay for my extravagance, the milk, arguing that even a wanderer on his feet was better able to spare a peseta than a village chief on his back. But he roared "No!" again, and furthermore commanded his wife to cut me a wedge of the longevious bread, "to carry me over the day."

Once escaped from the tangle of inhabited stone-piles, I strode away down rock-jumbled ravines, one close succeeding another and carrying me all but headlong downward. In the depths of the third I risked a plunge into a mountain brook, though the water was icy and the air still almost wintry cold. The day was warming, however, by the time I descended upon the hamlet of Berducedo, where I got fried eggs and a new highway.

To chronicle the vagaries of the latter during the rest of the day would be a thankless task. For miles it wound around and upward, ever upward on the face of bare stony mountains like a spiral stairway to heaven. Then suddenly from each giddy height it dived headlong down into deep-wooded, fertile valleys; then up again round and round another mountain shoulder far beyond the last stunted shrub. Later in the day it took to rounding these peaks almost on the level, coming a score of times so close to itself that I could all but toss my bundle across, only to buckle back upon itself for miles around some narrow but apparently bottomless gulley.

Somewhere during the previous afternoon I had crossed the unmarked boundary between Galicia and the still more rugged kingdom of Asturias, to-day the province of Oviedo. A new style of architecture gradually became prevalent. The buildings were of two stories, the lower, of stone, housing the animals, while the dwelling proper was of wood and perched a foot or more above the lower story on four cone-shaped cornerstones, like some great awkward bird ready to take flight.

But for this peculiarity the village in which night overhauled me differed but little from that of the evening before, except in being many hundred feet nearer sea level. It was called San Fecundo. As before, my inquiry for an inn was each time answered by a terse " I don't know." I found the head man in good health, however,— a stalwart fellow little past thirty who was shoveling manure in his front yard. Yet so local is the dialect of every village in this region that I tried for some time in vain to make known my wants to him.

" Can't you speak Spanish, señor? " I cried out.

" No, señor," he replied like the report of a gun, and apparently angered at the allegation. We managed nevertheless by patience and repetition to establish communication between us, and I found out at last why my inquiry for a posada had evoked so surprising an answer. Public hostelries being unknown among them, the mountaineers understand the question " Is there an inn in town? " to mean " Do you suppose any resident will furnish me accommodations? "

The head man did in this case, in spite of my unfortunate blunder in calling him a gallego. So great is the sectionalism in these Cantabrian ranges that a man from one village deeply resents even being taken for a resident of another a mile distant; while the Asturians, a blending of the aboriginal Iberian and the Goth, in whose caves of Covadonga was kept alight the last flicker of Spanish liberty and Christianity, consider themselves free and independent hidalgos infinitely superior to the submissive gallego. There were in truth some noticeable differences of character and customs, that were to increase as I advanced.

We spent the evening in another ventless, smoky, fly-buzzing kitchen, though this time the fireplace gave a bit of blaze and from time to time the rugged faces of the eight or ten men, who had gathered at the invitation of the village leader, flashed visible. I entertained them with such stories of America as are most customary and popular on such occasions. This was no light task. Not only were there many words entirely indigenous to the village, but such Castilian as my hearers used would scarcely be recognized in Castille. The expression " Por allà " (over there) they reduced to " Pa cá "; " horse " was never " caballo," but either " cabalo " or " cabayo." Worst of all, the infinitive of the verb served indifferently for all persons and tenses. " Yo ir " might mean " I go," " I was going," " I shall go," " I should go " and even " I would have gone " and " I should be going."

Most taking of all the stories I could produce were those concerning the high buildings of New York. I had developed this popular subject at some length when a mountaineer interposed a question that I made out at length to be a query whether those who

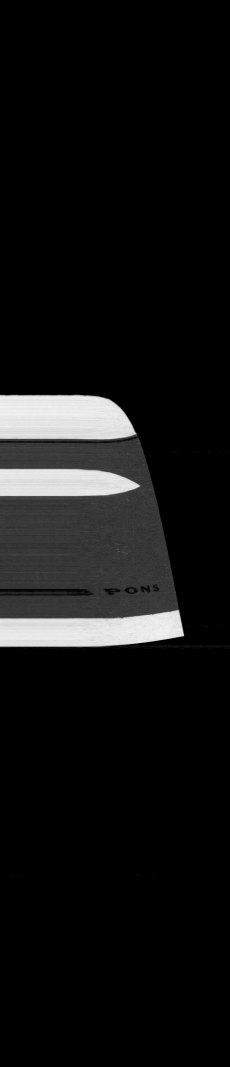

A bread market

Market women

live in these great houses spend all their time in them or take an hour or two every morning to climb the stairs.

"Hay ascensores, señores," I explained, "elevators; some expresses, some mixtos, as on your railroads."

A long, unaccountable silence followed. I filled and lighted my pipe, and still only the heavy breathing of the untutored sons of the hills about me sounded. Finally one of them cleared his throat and inquired in humble voice:

"Would you be so kind, señor, as to tell us what *is* an elevator?"

It was by no means easy. Long explanation gave them only the conception of a train that ran up and down the walls of the building. How this overcame the force of gravity I did not succeed in making clear to them; moreover there was only one of the group that had ever seen a train.

In the morning the head man accepted with some protest two *reales* — half a peseta. The highway again raced away downward, describing its parabolas and boomerang movements as before, and gradually bringing me to a realization of how high I had climbed into the sky. On every hand rocky gorges and sheer cliffs; now and again a group of charcoal-burners on the summit of a slope stood out against the dull sky-line like Millet's figures — for the sun was rarely visible. As I descended still lower, more pretentious, red-roofed villages appeared, and by mid-afternoon I entered the large town of Tineo. As I was leaving one of its shops a courtly youth introduced himself as a student in the University of Valladolid, and as he knew a bit of English it was with no small difficulty that I resisted his entreaties to talk that tongue with him in the mile or two he walked with me. That night for the first time since leaving Lugo I paid for my lodging in a public posada.

Salas, a long town in a longer green valley, was so far down and sheltered that figs sold — by number here rather than weight — nine for a cent. Beyond, the highway strolled for miles through orchards of apples and pears, while figs dropped thick in the road and were trodden under foot. For the first time I understood the force of the expression, " not worth a fig."

In the wineshop where I halted for an afternoon lunch I got the shock of that summer's journey. Casually I picked up the first newspaper I had seen in a week; and stared a full moment at it unbelieving. The entire front page was taken up by a photograph showing Posadas lying in bed, his familiar face gaunt with pain, and about him his father, a priest, and a fellow-torero.

" Carajo! " I gasped. " What 's this; Posadas wounded? "

" Más," replied the innkeeper shortly. " Killed

last Sunday. Too bad; he made good sport for the aficionados."

An accompanying article gave particulars. The Sevillian had been engaged to alternate with a well-known diestro in the humble little plaza of San Lucar de Barrameda on the lower reaches of the Guadalquivir. The end of the day would have seen him a graduate matador. The bulls were " miúras " five years old. As he faced the first, Posadas executed some pass that delighted the spectators. For once, evidently, he forgot his one " secret of success "; he turned to acknowledge the applause. In a flash the animal charged and gored him in the neck. He tried to go on, poised his sword, and fainted; and was carried to the little lazaret beneath the amphitheater, while the festival continued. Toward morning he died.

All this had passed while I was climbing into the cloud-cloaked village of Fonsagrada, two weeks to an hour since I had last seen the skilful Sevillian in the ring. The article ended with the vulgarity common to the yellow journal tribe:

" We have paid the dying Posadas one thousand pesetas for the privilege of taking this picture, which is almost all the unfortunate torero left his sorrowing family."

I trudged on deep in such reflections as such occurrences awaken, noting little of the scene. At sunset I found myself tramping through a warmer, less

abrupt country, half conscious of having passed
Grado, with its palaces, nurse-girls, and conventional
costumes. As dusk fell I paused to ask for an inn.
" A bit further on," replied the householder. I continued, still pensive. Several times I halted, always
to receive the same reply, " A bit further, señor."
Being in no sense tired, I gave the matter little attention until suddenly the seventh or eighth repetition of the unveracity aroused a touch of anger and
a realization that the night was already well advanced.
A lame man hobbling along the dark road gave me
once more the threadbare answer, but walked some
two miles at my side and left me at the door of a
wayside wineshop that I should certainly not have
missed even without him.

The chief sources of the boisterousness within were
three young vagabonds who were displaying their ac-
complishments to the gathering. One was playing
tunes on a comb covered with a strip of paper, another produced a peculiarly weird music in a high
falsetto, while the third was a really remarkable imi-
tator of the various dialects of Spain. With the
three I ascended near midnight to the loft of the
building, where a supply of hay offered comfortable
quarters. For an hour he of the falsetto sat smoking cigarettes and singing an endless ditty of his
native city, the refrain of which rang out at frequent intervals :

" Más bonita que hay,
A Zaragoza me voy
Dentro de Ar-r-r-rago-o-ón."

It was with genuine regret that I noted next morning the reapproach of civilization. Rough as is the life of these mountaineers of the north their entire freedom from convention, the contact with real men who know not even what pose and pretense are, the drinking into my lungs of the exhilarating mountain air had made the trip that was just ending by far the most joyful portion of all my Spanish experiences. Not since the morning I climbed into Astorga had I heard the whine of a beggar; not once in all the northwest had I caught the faintest scent of a tourist. The trip had likewise been the most inexpensive, for in the week's tramp I had spent less than twelve pesetas.

A few hours more down the mountainside brought me into Oviedo, where I took up my abode in the Calle de la Luna. The boyhood home of Gil Blas is a sober, almost gloomy town, where the sun is reputed to shine but one day in four. Its inhabitants have much in common with the slow-witted Lugense, though they are on the whole more wide-awake and self-satisfied. Of window displays the most frequent was that of a volume in richly illustrated paper cover entitled, " Los Envenenadores (poisoners) de

16

Chicago." It was, possibly, an exposé of the packing houses, but I did not find time to read it. August was nearing its close, and there was still a considerable portion of Spain to be seen. Luckily my kilometer-book was scarcely half-used up; but of the joyful days of freedom on the open road there could not be many more.

CHAPTER XIII

THE LAND OF THE BASQUE

MY knapsack garnished, I turned my back on Oviedo early on Sunday morning. The train wound slowly away toward the lofty serrated range that shuts off the world on the south. As we approached the mountains, the line began to tie itself in knots, climbing ever upward. In one section two stations seven miles apart had twenty-six miles of railroad between them. At the second of the two a flushed and puffing Spaniard burst into our compartment with the information that, having reached the former after the train had departed, he had overtaken us on foot.

Still we climbed until, at the turning of the day, high up where clouds should have been we surmounted the ridgepole of the range and, racing, roaring downward, were almost in a moment back in the barren, rocky, sun-baked Spain of old, dust swirling everywhere, the heat wrapping us round as with a woolen blanket, drying up the very tobacco in my pouch; a change almost as decided as from the forests of Norway to the plains of India.

Arrived in León at three, I set off at once tourist-fashion for the cathedral, with its soaring Gothic towers and delicate, airy flying-buttresses the first truly inspiring bit of Christian architecture I had seen in Spain; the first indeed whose exterior was anything. Much of the edifice, however, was glaringly new, the scaffolds of the renovators being still in place.

But here again " if the house of God is rich that of man is poor," pauperous in fact. When once the traveler has forced himself to believe that León was not many centuries since the rich capital of a vast empire he must surely fall sad and pensive reflecting how mutable and fleeting indeed are the things of earth. The León of to-day is a large village, a dried-up, dirty, dilapidated, depopulated, cobble-streeted village of snarling, meretricious-minded inhabitants jumbled together inside a wall that with the cathedral is the only remaining proof of former importance. Here once more was the beggar with his distressing whine, his brow of bronze, and his all too evident injuries; not numerously but constituting a large percentage of the population. In all Spain the devise of insurance companies on the fronts of buildings is more than frequent; in León there was barely a hovel without one or more. Which could not but awaken profound wonder, for not only are there no wooden houses within her walls to make danger of fire imminent, but a greater blessing could

The Roman walls of Leon

hardly be imagined for León than a general and all-embracing conflagration.

It was, perhaps, because of the unbroken misery with which they were surrounded that the Leonese were individually crabbed and cynical. Not a courteous word do I remember having received in all the town, and in vitriolic remarks the keepers and guests of the tumble-down parador where I was forced to put up outdid all others.

I was off in the morning at the first opportunity, again by train, which, passing in the early afternoon through a blinding sand-storm near the village of Cisneros, landed me soon after at Palencia. This was a counterpart of León; a trifle less sulky and universally miserable, but as sprawling, sun-parched, and slovenly. Its surrounding plains were utterly verdureless, their flanking hills ossified, its gardens, promenades, and Alameda past all hope of relief by sprinkling even had its river not long since gone desert-dry as the rest. I left the place quickly, riding into the night and descending at length to march to the inspiriting music of a military band along a broad, thick-peopled Alameda, at the end of which a giant statue of Columbus bulked massive against the moonlit sky, into Valladolid.

I had come again upon a real city, almost the first since leaving Madrid; whence accommodations, while in no sense lacking, were high in price. In the course of an hour of prowling, however, I was

apprised of the existence of a modest casa de
huéspedes in a canyon-like side street. I rang the
great doorbell below several times in vain; which was
as I had expected, for foolish indeed would have
been the Spaniard who remained within doors on
such a night, while the band played and the city
strolled in the Alameda. I dropped my bundle at
my feet and leaned against the lintel of the massive
doorway.

Within an hour there arrived another seeker after
quarters, a slender Spaniard in the early summer of
life, who carried two heavy portmanteaus and a
leather swordcase. Almost at the opening of our
conversation he surprised me by inquiring, "You are
a foreigner, verdad, señor?" I commended his pene-
tration and, as we chatted, sought for some sign of his
profession or place in society. All at once the long,
slender swordcase caught my eye.

"Ah! Es usted torero, señor," I observed with
assurance.

The youth awakened the echoes of the narrow
street with his laughter.

"Bullfighter! No, indeed! I am happy to say
no. I am a student in the national cavalry school
here, just returned from my month's furlough.
But your error is natural," he went on, "and my
fault. I have really no right to appear in civilian
garb. It would mean a month of bread and water
at least if one of our officers caught a glimpse of

me. But carajo! The family above may not be
back by midnight. We can leave our baggage with
the portier next door."

We strolled slowly back to the brilliantly lighted
Plaza de la Constitutión. Suddenly the youth interrupted an anecdote of the tan-bark to exclaim in a
calm but earnest voice:

"Caramba! There come my commandante and
the first lieutenant."

Two men of forty-five or fifty, in resplendent uniforms and tall red caps, their swords clinking along
the pavement, were sauntering down upon us. I
stepped quickly to the opposite side of my companion, being taller — and likewise curious.

"Hombre!" he protested sharply, stepping back
again. "No tenga V. cuidado. It is not our way
to hide from our officers."

With head erect and military stride he marched
straight on before him. Luckily the officers were so
engrossed in conversation that neither glanced up
as they passed.

We drifted into a café and ordered "helado," that
Spanish imitation of ice-cream the calling of which
in the streets had so frequently caused me to whirl
about in astonishment, so much does it sound like our
"hello." Over it we fell to discussing things American, in which we were gradually joined by several
well-dressed men at the adjoining marble tables. In
the course of the evening I chanced to remark that

one of the surprises of my summer's trip had been to find so little resentment against the United States.

"Señor," said the youth, while each and all of our companions gave signs of agreement, "nothing more fortunate has befallen our country in a century than the loss of Cuba and the Philippines. Not only has it taken a load off the Spanish people; it has brought more relief than you can guess to us of the army. The colonies were the dumping-ground of our profession. Once let an officer show ability and he was forthwith shipped off to the islands to die. Now they are taken away, Spain has already begun to regain her lost place among the nations. No, señor; we of the army at least think nothing but kindness to your people for the relief."

Returned to the casa de huéspedes, the student and I were given adjoining rooms and saw much of Valladolid together before I took train the second morning after to Burgos. There, were regulation "sights" in abundance; on every hand memories of the Cid Campeador, even the spot where stood his dwelling — all as authentic as the popular landmarks of Jerusalem. Two miles or more out along the shallow mill-race that Burgos calls a river I visited the nunnery of Las Huelgas, which claims for its distinction never in its centuries of existence to have admitted to the veil less than a daughter of the nobility. The stroll is pleasant, but the place, noble though it be, unexciting — at least outwardly. Of

the cathedral, the finest in Spain, much might be said
— that has been often said before.

It was in Burgos that I saw for the first time what
I might have seen earlier and frequently had my
tastes run that way,—a Spanish cemetery. More
exactly it was a corpse-file, a perpendicular hillside
in which hundreds of bodies had been pigeon-holed
for future reference, with the name and a charitably
indulgent characterization of the deceased on the
end of his coffin. The Spaniard, with his superstitions, prefers this style of tomb for much the same
reason, it seems, that the Arab seals his graves with
cement,— that the emissaries from the less popular
regions may not bear away the departed before the
agents of the better and hence slower realm put in an
appearance.

The greatest experience of my day in Burgos was
the view from the summit of the hot, dry Cerro de San
Miguel. Not merely does it offer a mighty and
comprehensive vista of half the stony-bare face of
Castilla Vieja, but a bird's-eye view as it were of all
Spain and her history. Of the city spread out at
one's feet fully three-fourths the space is taken up
by cathedral, churches, convents, monasteries, casas
de misericordia, the vast bulk of the castle, the barracks, the bullring,— all the countless buildings of
non-producers; while between them in the nooks and
corners wherever a crack offers are packed and huddled the hovels of the mere inhabitants. There, in

plain sight, is Spain's malady. She is a land of non-producers. Ecclesiastics, soldiers, useless octroi guards, beggars rotten with the notion fostered by the omnivorous priesthood that mendicancy is an honorable profession, make up almost the bulk of her population of productive age. Not without reason does nomadic Borrow lift up his clench-fisted wail against " Batuschca."

There is one road to redemption for Spain,—that she shoot her priests and set her soldiers to work. As isolated individuals the merry, dissolute fellows of the cloth might be permitted to live on as they have, and suffer the natural end of such living. But as a class they are beyond reform; their point of view is so utterly warped and incorrigible, they have grown so pestiferous with laziness and " graft " that there is no other remedy, " no hay otro remedio " as the Spaniard himself would say could his throttled mind cast off the rubbish of superstition and cant for one clear thought. Let him who protests that they are teachers of the youth go once and see what they teach,— the vapid, senseless lies about " saints " so far from truth as to be an abomination, so far above the possible aspirations and attainments of real humanity as to force the rising generations from very hopelessness of imitation to lose heart and sink to iniquity as the priesthood has done before them. Or are there some who still credit them with feeding the poor? A high praise, indeed, exactly

equal to that due the footpad who refunds his victim
carfare that he may be the more quickly rid of him.

Therein lies the chief weakness of Spain.   It is not
because she is ruled by a slender youth chosen by the
accident of birth rather than by a more portly man
chosen more or less by his fellow-citizens; not because her religion happens to be that of Rome rather
than the austerities of Calvin or the fatalism of Mo-
hammed; not because her national sport is a bit more
dramatically brutal than that of other lands; not
because her soil is dry and stony and her rains and
rivers slight; not because her people are decadent,
her human stock run down — I have plowed in the
sea in the foregoing pages if I have not made it clear
that her real manhood, the workman, the peasant, the
arriero, the muscle and sinew of the nation, are as
hardy, toilsome and all-enduring as the world harbors.   But in the long centuries of warfare her attention was drawn away from internal affairs, she fell
among thieves within, and the force of example, the
helplessness of the individual drove her people in the
line of least resistance,—to become thieves too, na-
tionally, officially, until mad grab-what-you-can-and-
the-devil-grab-the-ungrabbing has her by the throat
gasping for life.   If she is not to sink down for
the vultures of the nations to pick clean of her
meager scraps of flesh there must arise within her
boundaries a man, a movement, a sweeping change
that shall cast off the burden of precedent and turn

her officials to doing honestly with all their might what now they do with all their might dishonestly. She must regain confidence in the necessity and prevalence of honesty. She must learn that patent yet rarely comprehended truth that work and work only is the real source of life; she must cease to be the sworn enemy of the innovator, thinking her ways best and those of the rest of the world abnormal, unable to see a yard beyond her national boundaries, scorning all ideas and arguments from the outside like the most hide-bound of Orientals.

The next afternoon found me in Vitoria, in the land of the Basque; yet another kind of Spain. Vitoria is a city of to-day, clean, bustling, almost American in her streets and architecture and the wide-awake air of the *Vascongado*. The *boína* — round cap without visor and the end of a string for tassel — had all at once become universal, worn, like the fez in Damascus, by every age and grade of man from bootblack to mayor. So pleasing was this prosaic city that even though her prices were high I loitered in her shade until the next afternoon before seeking out the highway to Bilbáo.

There lay sixty-seven kilometers to the seaport, a half of which I hoped to cover before halting for the night. For on the following day Bilbáo was to celebrate in honor of the king. The way led me through a country fertile for all its stoniness, made so by the energy and diligence of the Basque, whose

View of Burgos from the Cerro de San Miguel

A donkey's siesta

strong features, bold curved nose, piercing eyes and sturdy form was to be seen on every hand. With the southern Spaniard this new race had almost nothing in common, and though as serious of deportment as the gallego there was neither his bashfulness nor stupidity. The Castilian spoken in the region was excellent, the farming implements of modern manufacture and the methods of the husbandman thousands of years ahead of Andalusia.

As the day was fading I began to clamber my way upward into the mountains that rose high in the darkening sky ahead. The night grew to one of the blackest, the heavens being overcast; but he who marches on into the darkness without contact with artificial light may still see almost plainly. It was two hours, perhaps, after nightfall, and the road was winding ever higher around the shoulder of a mammoth peak, its edge a sheer precipice above unfathomable depths, when suddenly I saw a man, a denser blackness against the sea of obscurity, standing stock-still on the utmost edge of the highway.

" Buenos tardes," I greeted in a low voice, almost afraid that a hearty tone would send him toppling backward to his death.

He neither answered nor moved. I stepped closer.

" You have rather a dangerous position, verdad, señor? "

Still he stared motionless at me through the darkness. Could he be some sleep-walker? I moved

quietly forward and, thrusting out a hand, touched
him on the sleeve. It was hard as if frozen! For
an instant I recoiled, then with a sudden instinctive
movement passed a hand quickly and lightly over his
face. Was I dreaming? That, too, was hard and
cold. I sprang back and, rummaging hastily
through my pockets, found one broken match. The
wind was rushing up from the bottomless gulf below.
I struck a light, holding it in the hollow of my hand,
and in the instant before it was blown out I caught
a few words of an inscription on a pedestal:

"ERECTED TO THE MEM —
THROWN OVER THIS PRECIPICE —
BANDITS — NIGHT OF —"

and before I had made out date or name I was again
in darkness.

Over the summit, on a lower, less wind-swept level,
I came upon a long mining town scattered on either
side of the highway. I dropped in at a wineshop
and bespoke supper and lodging. A dish of the now
omnipresent bacalao was set before me, but for a time
the keeper showed strong disinclination to house a
wandering stranger falling upon him at this advanced hour.

The young woman who served me at table and answered the demands for wine of the half-dozen youth-
ful miners about me seemed strangely out of place
in such surroundings. Nothing was plainer than

that she was not of the barmaid type. One would
have said rather the convent-reared daughter of some
well-to-do merchant or large farmer. This surmise
turned out to be close to the truth. When the carousing miners had drifted into the night and I, by dint
of talking and acting my best Castilian, had found
my way into the good graces of the family, I heard
the girl's story — for rightly approached the
Spaniard is easily led to talk of his private affairs.
Her father had been the principal shop-keeper of the
mining town, and had died a few weeks before. His
debts were heavy and when all claims had been settled there remained to his orphaned daughter five
hundred pesetas.

"But," I cried, "five hundred pesetas! It is a
fortune, señorita, in Spain. You could have started
a shop, or lived well until the novio appeared."

"Jesús María!" cried the girl, looking at me with
wondering eyes. "Do you forget purgatory? For
the repose of my father's soul five hundred masses
must be said; no less, the cura himself told me; and
each mass costs a peseta. Then I have come to work
here."

There was that in the air next morning that reminded me, as I wound down into a wooded, well-
peopled valley, that summer was drawing toward its
close. The day grew quickly warm, however. In the
knowledge that the king was sojourning in the city
upon which I was marching, I was fully prepared to

endure long catechizing and examination by guardias civiles. My wonder was not slight, therefore, when I was suffered to pass through one, two, three villages without being once challenged.

But the expected meeting came at last and quite made up for the lack of others. The third village lay already behind me when I heard an authoritative shout and, turning around, saw a bareheaded man of thirty, dressed half in peasant, half in village garb, beckoning to me with a commanding gesture to return. Fancying him some wily shop-keeper, I swung on my heel and set off again. He shouted loudly, and racing after me, caught me by an arm. I shook him off with an indignation that sent him spinning half across the highway. Instead of retreating he sprang at me again and we should certainly have been soon entangled in a crude performance of the manly art had he not cried out in a voice quaking with anger:

"Have a care, señor, in resisting the law. I am a miñón."

"Miñón!" I cried, recalling suddenly that in the Basque provinces the national guardias are reënforced by local officers thus named. "Then why the devil don't you wear your uniform? How shall I know you are not a footpad?"

"I shall prove that soon enough," he replied, still visibly shaking with the rage of a Spaniard whose "pundonor" has been sullied.

Saintly generosity—Murillo

I returned with him to the casa de ayuntamiento, in the doorway of which he halted, and, examining me for concealed weapons, demanded that I untie my knapsack. Never before had this been more than superficially inspected, but the thoroughness with which the angry miñón overhauled it, examining even my letters and fingering my clothes-brush over and over as if convinced that it could be opened by some secret spring, fully made up for any possible carelessness of his fellow-officers elsewhere. When he had lost hope of finding evidence of treason he handed back my possessions reluctantly and bade me with a scowl the conventional " Go with God; " to which I answered, " Queda V. con el mismísimo diablo "— but the thrust was too subtle for his bullet-headed intellect.

Toward noon the green slopes and cool forests turned to a cindered soil and the sooty aspect of a factory town. I mounted a last hill and descended quickly through a smoke-laden atmosphere into Bilbáo. Here was the first entirely modern city I had seen in Spain; one might easily have fancied one's self in Newcastle or Seattle. The Spanish casa de huéspedes seemed not even known by name, and in its place were only boisterous taverns, smacking of sea-faring custom and overrun with the touts that feed on the simple mariner.

As I sat toward evening in one of these establishments, there entered a man something over thirty-five,

17

dressed in boína and workingman's garb that showed
but slight wear.   I noted him only half consciously,
being at that moment expressing to the landlord my
surprise that the king, instead of being in Bilbáo as
he was reported by the newspapers, was ten or twelve
miles away on his yacht at the mouth of the river.
The keeper, a stocky Basque of much better parts
than the average of his guild, glanced up from his
spigots and replied in a smooth and pleasant voice:

"Porque, señor, no quiere morir tan joven — Because he does not care to die so young."

"Y con mujer tan bella y fresca — And with a wife
so beautiful and fresh," added a thick-set fellow at
a neighboring table without looking up from his
cards.

Love for Alfonso is not one of the characteristics
of the masses in this section of the country.

Meanwhile the newcomer, whose eye had been
wandering leisurely over the assembly, threaded his
way half across the room to sit down at my table.   I
wondered a bit at the preference, but certain he was
no tout, gave him the customary greeting.   By the
time I had accepted a glass and treated in turn we
were exchanging personal information.   He announced himself a cobbler, and even before I had
broached the subject suggested that he could find me
a lodging with an old woman above his shop.   This
workroom, when we reached it, proved to be nothing
but a kit of tools and a few strips of leather scat-

tered about the small hallway at the foot of the stairs. I found above the hospitality he had promised, however, and paying two night's lodging in an unuusually pleasant room, descended.

The shoemaker appeared more obliging than industrious, for he at once laid aside the shoe he was hammering and announced that he was going to give himself the pleasure of spending the evening with me and of finding me the best place to take in the fireworks that were to be set off in honor of the king. I explained that it was rather my plan to attend the city theater, where I might both see that remarkable personage in the flesh and hear one of Molière's best comedies in Spanish.

" There is more than time for both," replied the cobbler, and forthwith fell to extolling the coming spectacle so highly that he came near to arousing within me, too, an interest in the fireworks.

At the end of an hour's stroll we found ourselves on the summit of a knoll in the outskirts, in a compact sea of Bilbaoans watching a tame imitation of a Fourth of July celebration on the slope of one of the surrounding hills. The display was, as I have said, in honor of the king; though it turned out that his indifferent majesty was at that moment dining and wining a company of fellow-sportsmen on board the *Giralda* twelve miles away.

The cobbler set a more than leisurely pace back to the city, but we regained at length the bank of the river and, crossing the wooded Paséo Arenal, approached the theater.   Before it, was packed a vast and compact multitude through which I struggled my way to the entrance, only to be informed in the customary box-office tones that there was not another ticket to be had.   The shoemaker was no theatergoer, and as my own disappointment was not overwhelming, we set out to fight our way back to the Paséo.

Long before we had succeeded in that venturesome undertaking, however, there burst forth a sudden, unheralded roar of uncounted voices, the immense throng surged riverward with an abruptness that all but swept us off our feet, the thunder of thousands of hoofs swelled nearer, and down upon us rode an entire regiment of guardias civiles in uniforms so new they seemed but that moment to have left the tailor, and astride finer horses than I had dreamed existed in Spain.   Straight into the crowd they dashed, headlong, at full canter, like cowboys into a drove of steers, sweeping all before them, scattering luckless individuals in all directions, and completely surrounding the theater in solid phalanx. Before I had recovered breath there arose another mighty shout, and, some three hundred more horsemen, with a richly caparisoned carriage in their midst, dashed through the throng from a landing-stage on the river bank behind us to the door of the theater. I caught a fleeting glimpse of a slight figure in a

The land of the boina

Alfonso XIII at a picnic

rakish overcoat, a burst of music sounded from the theater, and died as suddenly away as the doors closed behind the royal arrival. Again the cavalry charged, driving men, women and children pellmell back a hundred yards from the building and, forming a yet wider circle around it, settled down to sit their horses like statues until the play should be ended.

When my wonder had somewhat subsided there came upon me an all but uncontrollable desire to shout with laughter. The ludicrousness, the ridiculousness of it all! A vast concourse of humanity driven helter-skelter like as many cattle, scores of persons jostled and bruised, thirteen hundred of the most able-bodied men in Spain to sit motionless on horseback around a theater late into the night, all for the mere protection of one slight youth whose equal was easily to be found in every town or village of the land! Truly this institution of kingship is as humorous a hoax as has been played upon mankind since man was.

A hoax on all concerned. For the incumbent himself, the slender youth inside, who must spend his brief span of years amid such mummery, commands of himself a bit of mild admiration. I fell to wondering what he would give for the right to wander freely and unnoticed all a summer's day along the open highway. Let him who can imagine himself born a king, discovering as early as such notions can penetrate to his infant intellect that his fellow-

mortals have placed him high on a pedestal, have
given him even without the asking power, riches,
and almost reverence as a superior being, when at
heart he knows full well he is of quite the same clay
as they; and he may well ask himself whether he would
have grown up even as manly as the youth who goes
by the name of Alfonso XIII. Recalling that former kings of Spain could not be touched by other than
a royal finger, we may surely grant common sense
to this sovereign who dances uncondescendingly with
daughters of the middle class, who chats freely with
bullfighters, peasants, or apple-women. Pleasing,
too, is his devil-may-carelessness. On this same
night, for instance, after reboarding his yacht, he
took it suddenly into his mad young head to return
at once through this, his most hostile province, to his
queen. At one in the morning he was rowed ashore
with one companion, stepped into his automobile,
himself playing chauffeur, and tore away through
Bilbáo and a hundred miles along the craggy coast
to San Sebastián. It is not hard to guess what
might have happened had he punctured a tire among
those stony mountains and been chanced upon by
a homing band of peasants brave with wine.

Musing all which I turned to address the cobbler and found him gone. The crowd was slowly
melting away. I sat down in the Paséo and waited an
hour, but my erstwhile companion did not reappear.
When I descended from my lodging next morning

there remained not a trace of his " shop " at the foot of the stairs. Had the village miñón done me the honor of telegraphing my description to the seaport, or was my road-worn garb the livery of suspicion? This only I know; when, that Sunday evening after my return from a glimpse of the open sea, I asked my hostess whether her fellow renter were really a shoemaker, she screwed up her parchment-like features into a smile and answered:

" Si, señor, one of the shoemakers of his majesty."

CHAPTER XIV

A DESCENT INTO ARAGÓN

THERE was an unwonted excitement in the air when I boarded the train next morning for the longest unbroken ride of my Spanish journey. Pernales, the anachronism, the twentieth-century bandit of the environs of Córdoba, had fallen. Aboard the train newspapers were as numerous as on the New York "Elevated" at a similar hour. I bought one and was soon lost like the rest in the adventures of this last defier of the mighty guardia civil.

The story was simple. Two evenings before, about the time I had been yawning over the king's fireworks, Pernales had met a village arriero among the foothills of his retreat, and asked him some question about the road. The rustic gave him the desired information, but guessing with whom he was speaking, had raced away, once he was out of sight, as fast as he could drive his ass before him, to carry his suspicions to the village alcalde. The rest was commonplace. A dozen guardias stalked the unsuspecting bandolero among the hills, and coming upon him toward sunrise, brought his unsanctioned career abruptly to a close.

"Our special correspondent" had dismally failed
to cast over his account the glamour of romance, but
in compensation had taken a reporter's care to give
the precise point in the right temple where the ball
had entered, with the exact dimensions of the orifice,
as well as the life story of the hero who had bored
it. Nay, with almost American haste and resource-
fulness the paper printed a full-length portrait of
the successful hunter — or one at least of a man who
could not have been vastly different in appearance,
in a uniform that was certainly very similar. Alas!
The good old days of the bandit and the contraban-
dista are forever gone in Spain; the humdrum era of
the civil guard is come. Pernales' is but another
story of a man born a century too late.

All day long as we toiled and twisted over the
Cantabrian range and descended southward, this only
was the topic of conversation of all grades and sexes
of travelers. An hour's halt at Miranda and we
creaked on along the bank of Spain's greatest river,
the Ebro, talking still of bandoleros and the regret
of their passing. Slowly the green tinge in the landscape faded away and in its place came reddish cliffs
and a sun-seared and all but desert country spreading away from either bank of the red-dyed river,
sterile rolling plains relieved only by small oases of
fertility and isolated and in all probability bigoted
villages standing colorless on colorless hillsides. As
central Spain may be likened to rocky Judea, so this

resembles in some degree Egypt, with the Ebro as the Nile.

It was late in the evening when I arrived in Saragossa and, crossing the broad river by the Puente de Piedra, found myself in one of the most labyrinthian cities of Spain. But so practiced had I grown in such quest that in less than an hour I had engaged accommodation at my own price, which by this time had descended to two and a half pesetas.

The "sight" par excellence of Saragossa is of course her "Virgen del Pilar." The story runs that Santiago, who is none other than Saint James, while wandering about Spain, as he was wont to ramble in various corners of the earth, was favored one evening by a call from the Mother of Christ, who, during all their little chat, stood on the top of a stone pillar. That the tale is true there seems little chance for doubt, for they have the pillar yet; and it is over this that has been erected the vast cathedral to which flock thousands of pilgrims during every month of the year.

I repaired to it early, but was soon turned melancholy with the recollection of Puck's profound saying anent the folly of mankind. The interior of the edifice is as impressive as that of an empty warehouse. Under the main dome is a large chapel screaming with riches, in the back of which, on her pillar, stands the Virgin — turned to black, half-decayed wood — dressed in more thousands of dollars' worth of gold and silver, of resplendent robes and vociferous gaudiness than god Juggernaut of India ever possessed at the height of his influence. Before it worshipers are always kneeling. In the back wall of the chapel is an opening through which one can touch the pillar — and find a cup-shaped hole worn in it by such action during the centuries. I sat down on a bench near the far-famed orifice, and for close upon an hour watched the unbroken procession file past. Beggar women, rag-pickers, ladies of wealth, cankerous old men, merchants, city sports, lawyers — Saragossa is the one city of Spain where even men go to church — every grade and variety of Aragonese pressed close upon the heels one of another, each bowing down as he passed to kiss the hole deeper into the pillar. At bottom the difference is slight indeed between the religion of the Spaniard and that of the Hindu.

In the city swarms a hungry, ragged people, more often than not without shoes, yet one and all with the proverbial haughty pride and somber mood of Aragón in face and bearing, stiff-shouldered, bristling with a touch-me-not-with-a-pole expression. Here, too, may still be found, especially among the peasants from the further districts, the old provincial costume,— knee breeches, a jacket reaching barely to the waist, and a red cloth wound about the head.

Tiring of such things, there is a pleasant promenade along the banks of the Ebro, whence one will drift naturally through the Portillo gate where the

"flying Gaul was foil'd by a woman's hand." It is
startling to find the settings of two such world-famed
dramas so close together, but from the gate one has
only to saunter a few yards along the Madrid highway to come upon the weather-battered Aljafería
of "Trovatore" fame. To-day it is a barracks.
Within its towers, through now unbarred windows,
may be seen soldiers polishing their spurs and muskets, humming now and then a snatch of popular
song; but one may wait in vain to hear some tuneful
prisoner strike up the expected "miserere."

There is one stroll in Saragossa that I would com-
mend to the wanderer who finds pleasure in gaining
elevations whence he may look down, as it were, on
the world. It is out along the Canal Imperial, past
the swollen-paunched statue of its sponsor Pignatelli,
and across the Huerva; then winding lazily southwest
and upward the stroller comes suddenly out on the
crown of a bald hillock. There, below him in its flat
valley, spreads all Saragossa, far enough away to
lose the crassness of detail, yet distinct, the two
finished towers of the Pilar rising above it like mina-
rets, the whole girded by the green huerta, and beyond and all around the desert in gashed and gnarled
hills like the Libyan range of another continent.
Here I lounged until the setting sun, peering over
my shoulder, cast the radiant flush of evening on the
city below, which gradually fading away was at
length effaced in the night, its sounds mingling to-

A typical Spanish street

Wash-day

of rocky hillside farming. Of both his province of Navarre and of himself he talked freely until suddenly my tongue stumbled upon some question of military conscription. He fell at once silent, his jaws stiffened, and into his face came the reflection of a bitter sadness. For the Basques are by no means reconciled to the loss of their cherished *fueros*, or special political privileges. In silence the sturdy old man led the way half across the city to one of her gates and, climbing a knoll that gave a good view of the surrounding fortifications, said in cheerless tones:

" Don Henrico, we have here the strongest city walls in Spain. But what use are they now against the king's modern artillery? No hay remedio. We must serve in his armies."

As we threaded our way slowly back to the boarding-house I halted at a money changer's to buy a twenty-franc piece. The transaction left me only a handful of coppers in Spanish currency, and I went early to bed lest there be not enough remaining to carry me out of the country.

On a glorious clear September morning I turned my back on Spain and set forth from Pamplona to tramp over the Pyrenees by the pass of Roncesvalles, being just uncertain enough of the road to lend zest to the undertaking. At the edge of the plain to the northward of the city a highway began to wind its way upward along the bank of a young river, not

laboriously, but steadily rising. Habitations were
rare. Late in the morning a spot above whirling
rapids in shaded solitude suggested a plunge; but as
I pulled off my coat a sound fell on my ear and, looking across the stream, I saw a half-dozen women kneeling on the bank and staring curiously across at me.
When I retreated, they laughed heartily and fell once
more to pounding away at their laundry-work on the
stones.

Some distance higher I found another pool in
which, by rolling over and over, I won the afterglow
of a real swim. Sharper ascents succeeded, though
still none steep. I was soon surrounded by a Tyrol-
ian scenery of forest and deep-cut valleys, and among
up-to-date people — the farming implements being of
modern type and the smallest villages having electric
lights run by power from the mountain streams.
Every fellow-mortal, young or old, as is usual in
mountain regions, gave me greeting, not with the
familiar " Vaya! " nor the " Buenos! " of Galicia,
but with "Adiós! " which seemed here to mean much
more than the grammatical " Good-by." In the
place of guardias civiles were carabineros in a provincial uniform, whose advances, if less warm and
companionable, were none the less kindly.

Toward evening the road flowed up into a broad,
oblong meadow, ankle-deep in greenest grass, musical
with the sound of cow-bells, across which it drifted as
if content to rest for a time on its oars before taking

A guardia civil and an "aficionado"

The baker makes his morning round

the final climb. The sun was setting when I reached Burguete at forty-four kilometers, station of the trans-Pyrenean diligence and the point that I had been assured I should do well to reach in a two-day's walk. But I felt as unwearied as at the outset; the towers of Roncesvalles stood plainly visible five kilometers ahead across the green tableland. I rambled on in the cool of evening and by dark was housed in a good inn of the mountain village.

When the supper hour arrived, the landlord stepped across to me to ask whether I would eat as a guest or as a member of the family. I inquired what the distinction might be.

" No difference," he answered, " except that as a member of the family you pay a peseta upon leaving, and as a guest you pay two."

It was of course en famille that I supped, and right royally, at a board merry with good-humored peasants and arrieros rather than in the silent, gloomy company of a half-dozen convention-ridden travelers in an adjoining room.

Roncesvalles would have been an unequaled spot in which to pass an autumn week, roaming in the forest glens of the mountains, dreaming of the heroic days of Roland. But the hour of reckoning and of New York was near at hand. Of all sensations I most abhor the feeling that I *must* be in a given place at a given time.

A short climb through wooded hillsides strewn with
18

gigantic rocks and I found myself all at once and unexpectedly on the very summit of the Pyrenees.   In
no sense had the ascent been toilsome, vastly less so
than several scrambles of two or three hours' dura-
tion between Lugo and Oviedo.   From the French
side, no doubt, it would have been far more of a task.
Gazing northward I recognized for the first time that
I stood high indeed above the common level of the
earth.   Miles below, blue as the sea, lay France, the
forested mountains at my feet rolling themselves out
into hills, the hills growing lower and lower and
spreading away into the far, far distance like another world.   The modern world — and I was all at
once assailed with a desire to ask what it had been doing in all the days I had been gone.   Then the highway seized me in its grasp and hurried me away
down, racing, rushing, almost stumbling, so fast I
was forced to break away from it and clamber down
at my own pace through dense unpeopled forests, to
fall upon it again far below and stalk with it at lunch-
time into the village of Val Carlos.   Yet another
hour's descent and I crossed a small stream into the
little hamlet of Arneguy; the long-forgotten figure of
a French gendarme slouched forth from a hut to
shout as I passed, " Anything dutiable, monsieur? "
and my Spanish journey was among the things that
have been.

CHAPTER XV

IN reality almost as much as in fancy I had entered another world. It is chiefly in retrospect that a journey through Spain, as through Palestine, brings home to the traveler the full difference between those gaunt regions of the earth and the world to which he is accustomed. Here the change was like that from a squatter's cabin, a bachelor's quarters to a residence of opulence.

Arrived while the day was still in its prime at St. Jean Pied de Port, I found myself undecided how to continue. The rescuing forty dollars awaited me — postal errors precluded — in Bordeaux; but Baedeker having now become mere lumber, I had no means of knowing which of two routes to follow to that city. I halted to make inquiries of an old Spaniard drowsing before his shop — so like one of mine own people he seemed amid this babble of French. But though he received me with Castilian courtesy he could give me no real information. Under the awning of a café a hundred paces beyond, two well-dressed men were sipping cooling drinks. Their

touring-car stood before the building, and not far
away, in the shade of an overhanging shoulder of the
Pyrenees, loitered a chauffeur, in all the accustomed
accoutrements of that genus. He had the appearance of an obliging fellow. I strolled across to him,
hastily summoning up my dormant French.

"Monsieur," I began, "vous me pardonnerez,
mais pour aller d'ici à Bordeaux vaut il mieux passer
par Bayonne ou bien par Mont de —"

He was grinning at me sheepishly and shifting
from one leg to the other. As I paused he blurted
out:

"Aw, I don't talk no French!"

"Then I suppose it 'll have to be English," I answered, in the first words of that language I had
spoken in ninety-six days — and in truth they came
with difficulty.

"Go' bly' me!" burst out the astounded knight of
the steering-wheel. "'Ow ever 'd you get in this
corner o' the world? Say, I ayn't said more 'n ' yes,
sir ' or ' no, sir ' to their lordships —" with a slight
jerk of the head toward the men under the awning
—" in so long I 've bally near forgot 'ow. 'Ere it
is Sunday an'—"

"Saturday," I interrupted.

"Sunday, I say," repeated the chauffeur, drawing
out a card on which were penciled many crude
crosses. "Ere 's 'ow I keep track —"

"Señora," I asked, turning to a woman who was

filling a pitcher at a hydrant behind me, " qué día tenemos hoy? "

Her lip curled disdainfully as she answered:

" Tiens! Vous me croyez un de ces barbares-là? " — tossing her head toward the mountain range behind us.

" Mille pardons," I laughed. " Force of habit. This monsieur and I are disputing whether to-day is Saturday or Sunday."

" Out again without your nurses! " she cried sarcastically. " Saturday, of course."

" Now 'ear that! " said the chauffeur, almost tearfully, when I interpreted. " 'Ow ever can a man keep track of anything in this bally country? Say, what was that question you was tryin' to ask me? "

" I 'm walking from Gib to Bordeaux," I remarked casually, and repeated my former inquiry. His expression changed slowly from incredulity to commiseration. Suddenly he thrust a hand into his pocket.

" I say, won't you 'ave a mite of a lift? Why, we took near all yesterday to come from that place. You could n't walk there in a month."

" No, thanks, I 'm fairly well heeled," I answered.

" Better 'ave a yellow-boy," he persisted, drawing out several English sovereigns. " Lord, you 're more 'n welcome, y' know. They ayn't no bloomin' use to me 'ere! "

At that moment I noted that the milords under the

awning had spread out before them a large touring map, and I left the chauffeur gasping at my audacity as I stepped across to them. The older was struggling to give an order to the waiter, who crouched towel on arm over them. There is a strange similarity between a full-grown Briton attempting to speak French and a strong man playing with a doll.

" Beg pawdon, gentlemen," I said, when I had helped them out of the difficulty, " but would you mind my glancing at your map? I want to find —"

" Ah — why, certainly," gasped one of the startled nobles.

But even with the chart before me I was no nearer a decision, for the two roads appeared of almost equal length. As I turned away, however, a poster on a nearby wall quickly settled my plans. It announced a great bullfight in Bayonne the next afternoon, with Quinito, Mazzatinito, and Regaterín, among the most famous of Spain's matadores — far more so than any it had been my fortune to see in that country.

I sped away at once along a macadamed highway at the base of the Pyrenees beside a clear river — a mere " rivière " to the French, but one that would have been a mighty stream in Spain. Its banks were thickly grown with willows. On the other hand the mountain wall, no less green, rose sheer above me, bringing an unusually early sunset. Along the way I met several old men, all Basques, who noting

that I also wore the boína greeted me in their native
" Eúscarra." Not a word of any other tongue
could they speak; and when I shook my head hope-
lessly at their hermetical language, they halted to
gaze after me with expressions of deep perplexity.
So, too, in the mountain-top village of Bidarry to
which I climbed long after dark after a dip in the
river, all speech was Basque; though some of the
younger inhabitants, finding I was of their race only
from the cap upward, fell to talking to me in fluent
French or Spanish.

The first hours of the following day were in the
highest degree pleasant. Thereafter the country
grew hilly, the sun torrid, and as I was forced to
set the sharpest pace to reach the bullring by four.
I put in as dripping a half-day as at any time during the summer; and I have yet to be more nearly
incinerated in this life than in the sol of the great
" Place des Taureaux " of Bayonne, crushed between
a workman in corduroys and a Zouave in the thickest woolen uniform the loom weaves.

The fight, like the ring, was Spanish in every
particular, though the programmes were printed in
French. It was by all odds the greatest córrida I
was privileged to attend during the summer, for the
three matadores stand in the front rank of their
profession. Yet it was somehow far less exhilarating than those I had seen in Spain. One had a feeling that these past masters were running far less

risk than their younger colleagues; one enjoyed their dexterity as one enjoys a seasoned public speaker, yet the performance lacked just the thrill of amateurishness.

Here, too, I saw Spain's greatest picador, the only one indeed I ever saw accomplish what the picador is supposed to do,— to hold off the bull with his *garrocha*. This he did repeatedly, placing his lance so unerringly that he stopped the animal's most furious charges and forced him to retire bellowing with rage and with blood trickling down over his shoulders. In all the afternoon this king of the pikepole had but one horse killed under him. It was in connection with this one fall that Quinito, the boldest of the matadores, won by his daring such applause as seemed to shake the Pyrenees behind us. Moreno lay half buried under his dead horse, in more than imminent danger of being gored to death by the bull raging above him. In vain the anxious caudrilla flaunted their cloaks. All at once Quinito stepped empty handed into the ring and caught the animal by the tail. Away the brute dashed across the plaza, twisting this way and that, but unable to bring his horns nearer than an inch or two of his tormentor who, biding his time, let go and vaulted lightly over the barrier.

I quitted Bayonne with the dawn and for four days following marched steadily on across the great *Landes* of France. Miles upon miles the broad highway stretched unswerving before me through an ultra-flat country between endless forests of pine. On the trunk of every tree hung a sort of flowerpot to catch the dripping pitch. There was almost no agriculture, nothing but pine-trees stretching away in regular rows in every direction, a solitude broken only by the sighing of the wind sweeping across the flatlands, where one could shout to the full capacity of one's lungs without awakening other response than long rolling echoes. Once in a while a pitch-gatherer flitted among the trees; less often the highway crossed a rusty and apparently trainless railroad at the solitary stations of which were tumbled hundreds of barrels of pitch.

My shoes wore out, those very oxfords " custom-made " in America and honestly tapped in Toledo, and I was forced to continue the tramp in al-pargatas, or what had here changed their name to *sandales*. As my twenty-franc piece melted away a wondering began to grow upon me whether I was really homeward bound after all; so myriad are the mishaps that may befall a mere letter.

Still the unswerving road continued, the endless forests stretched ahead. Such few persons as I met scowled at me in the approved French fashion, never once imitating the cheery greeting of the Spaniard. Now and again a man-slaughtering automobile tore by like some messenger to or from the infernal regions, recalling by contrast one of the chief charms of the land I had left behind. Hardly one of those destroyers of peace and tranquillity had I seen or heard in all Spain.

Four months afoot had not improved my outward appearance. It was not strange that the post-office officials of Bordeaux stared at me long and suspiciously when I arrived at length one afternoon with a single franc in my pocket. The letter was there. When I had, after the unwinding of endless red tape, collected the amount of the order, my journey seemed over indeed.

The " Agents Maritimes " to whom I applied accepted me readily enough as an emigrant to America, agreeing to pick me up in Bordeaux and set me down unstarved in New York for the net sum of two hundred and three francs. But there came a hitch in the proceedings. The agent was firing at me with Gaelic speed the questions prescribed by our exacting government —" Name? " " Age? " " Profession? "— and setting down the answers almost before I gave them, when:

" Have you contracted to work in the United States? "

" Oui, monsieur."

He stopped like a canvas canoe that has struck a snag.

" C'est impossible," he announced, closing his book of blanks with a thump. " We cannot of course sell you a ticket."

I plunged at once into an explanation. I advanced the information that the contract labor law was not framed to shut out American citizens. I protested that I had already toiled a year under the contract in question, and for my sins must return to toil another. I made no headway whatever.

" It is the law of the United States," he snapped. " Voilà! C'est assez."

Luckily I had a day to spare. By dint of appealing to every maritime authority in the city I convinced the agent at last of his error. But it was none too soon. With my bundle and ticket in one hand and a sort of meal-sack tag to tie in my lapel — if I so chose — in the other, I tumbled into the night train for Paris just as its wheels began to turn. Emigrant tickets are not good in France by day. There was one other tagged passenger in the compartment, a heavy-mannered young peasant likewise wearing a boína. Being thus drawn together we fell gradually into conversation. He was at first exceeding chary, with the two-fold canniness of the Basque and of the untraveled rustic whose native village has warned him for weeks to beware wily strangers. When I displayed my ticket, however, he lost at once his suspicion and, drawing out his own, proposed that we make the journey as partners. He was bound for Idaho. We did not, however, exchange ideas with partner-like ease, for though he had passed his twenty-five years in the province of Guipuzcoa he spoke little Spanish.

Near midnight a few passengers alighted and I fell into a cramped and restless sort of dog-sleep from which I awoke as we screamed into Versailles. When we descended at the Montparnasse station we were joined by three more Basques from another compartment. They, too, wore boínas and, like my companion, in lieu of coats, smocks reaching almost to the knees. They were from near Pamplona and had tickets from Bordeaux to Fresno, California, having taken this route to avoid the difficulties of leaving Spain by sea.

The Paris agent of the " American Line " did not meet us in silk hat and with open arms; but when we had shivered about the station something over an hour an unshaven Italian of forty, with lettered cap and a remarkable assortment of unlearned tongues picked us up and bore us away by omnibus to his " Cucina Italiana " in the Passage Moulin. Breakfast over, I invited my fellow-emigrants to view Paris under my leadership. They accepted, after long consultation, and we marched away along the Rue de Lyon to the site of the Bastille, then on into the roar of the city, the Spaniards so helplessly overwhelmed by the surrounding sights and sounds that I was called upon times without number to save them being run down. At length we crossed to the island and, the morgue being closed, entered Notre Dame.

I had hitherto credited Catholic churches with being the most democratic of institutions. Hardly were we inside, however, when a priest steamed down upon my companions.

"Sortez de suite!" he commanded. "Get out! How dare you enter the sacred cathedral in blouses!"

The Basques stared at him open-mouthed, now and then nervously wiping their hands on the offending smocks. I passed on and they followed, pausing where I paused, to gape at whatever I looked upon. The priest danced shouting about them. They smiled at him gratefully, as if they fancied he were explaining to them the wonders of the edifice. His commands grew vociferous.

"Ces messieurs, sir," I remarked at last, "are Spaniards and do not understand a word of French."

"You then, tell them to get out at once!" he cried angrily.

"You must pardon me, monsieur," I protested, "if I do not presume to appoint myself interpreter to your cathedral."

We continued our way, strolling down one nave to the altar, sauntering back along the other toward the entrance, the priest still prancing about us. In the doorway the Basques turned to thank him by signs for his kindness and backed away devoutedly crossing themselves.

At the Louvre, however, the smock-wearers were halted at the door by two stocky officials, and we wandered on into the Tuileries Gardens. There the quartet balked. These hardy mountaineers, accustomed to trudge all day on steep hillsides behind their burros, were worn out by a few miles of strolling on city pavements. For an hour they sat doggedly in a bench before I could cajole them a few yards further to the Place de la Concorde to board a Seine steamer and return to the Cucina. I left them there and returned alone to while away the afternoon among my old haunts in the Latin Quarter.

Soon after dark the razorless son of Italy took us once more in tow and, climbing to the imperial of an omnibus, we rolled away through the brilliant boulevards to the gare St. Lazare. Here was assembled an army of emigrants male and female, of all ages and various distances from their last soaping. In due time we were admitted to the platform. A third-class coach marked " Cherbourg " stood near at hand. I stepped upon the running-board to open a door. A station official caught me by the coat-tail with an oath and a violence that would have landed me on the back of my head but for my grip on the door handle. Being untrained to such treatment, I thrust out an alpargata-shod foot mule-fashion behind me. The official went to sit down dejectedly on the further edge of the platform. By and by he came back to shake his fist in my face. I spoke to him in his own tongue and he at once subsided, crying:

" Tiens! I thought you were one of those animals there."

We were finally stuffed into four cars, so close we were obliged to lie all night with our legs in one another's laps. The weather was arctic, and we slept not a wink. Early in the morning we disentangled moody and silent in Cherbourg. Another unshaven agent took charge of my companions' baggage with the rest, promising it should be returned the moment they were aboard ship. I clung skeptically to my bundle. We were herded together in a tavern and served coffee and bread, during the administration of which the agent collected our tickets and any proof that we had ever possessed them, and disappeared. The day was wintry cold. All the morning we marched shivering back and forth between the statue of Napoleon and the edge of the beach, the teeth of the south-born Basques chattering audibly. At noon we jammed our way into the tavern again for soup, beef and poor cider, and were given rendezvous at two at one of the wharves.

By that hour all were gathered. It was after four, however, when a tender tied up alongside. A man stepped forth with an armful of tickets and began croaking strange imitations of the names thereon. I heard at last a noise that sounded not altogether unlike my own name and, no one else chancing to forestall me, marched on board to reclaim my credentials. A muscular arm thrust me

on through a passageway in which a Frenchman in
uniform caught me suddenly by the head and turned
up my eyelids with a sort of stiletto.   Before I could
double a fist in protest another arm pushed me on.
At six a signal ran up, we steamed out through the
breakwater, and were soon tumbling up the gangway
of the steamer *New York*.   At the top another doctor lay in wait, but forewarned, I flung open my passport, and flaunting it in his face, stepped unmolested on deck.

Some four hundred third-class passengers had
boarded the steamer in England, and no small percentage of the berths were already occupied.   Unlike the nests of the *Prinzessin*, however, they might
reasonably be called berths, for though they offered
no luxury, or indeed privacy, being two hundred in a
section, the quarters were ventilated, well-lighted,
and to a certain extent clean.   I stepped to the nearest unoccupied bunk and was about to toss my bundle
into it when a young steward in shirt-sleeves and
apron sprang at me.

"No good, John," he shouted, in Cockney accents
and striving to add force to his remarks by a clumsy
pantomime.   "Berth take.   No more.   No good,
John.   All gone.   But —" jerking his head sidewise —"Pst! John!   I know one good berth.   One
dollar —" holding up a hand with forefinger and
thumb in the form of that over-popular object —
"All take, Joh —"

" Say, what t'ell 's the game, anyhow, mate? " I
interrupted.

His legs all but wilted under him.

" Sye, ol' man," he cried, patting me on the
shoulder. " S'elp me, I took you for one o' these
waps, as why should n't I, in that there sky-piece
an' make-up? Of course you can 'ave the berth.
Or sye, over 'ere by the port'ole's a far 'an'somer
one. There y' are. Now, mite, if ever I can 'elp
you out —" and he was still chattering when I
climbed again on deck.

Unfortunately, in the rough and tumble of em-
barking I had lost sight of the Spaniards. When I
found them again every berth was really taken, for
there was a shortage — or rather considerably more
than the legal number of tickets had been sold; and
the quartet, having withstood the blackmail, were
among those unprovided. That night they slept, if
at all, on the bare deck. Next day I protested to
the third-class steward and he spread for them two
sacks of straw on a lower hatch. There, too, the icy
sea air circulated freely. Worst of all, in spite of
the solemn promises of the agent, their bags, in which
they had packed not only blankets and heavier garments, but meat, bread, fruit, cheese, and botas of
wine sufficient to supply them royally during all the
journey, had been stowed away in the hold. For
two days they showed, after the fashion of emigrants, no interest in gastronomic matters. When

19

appetite returned they could not eat American —
or rather English food. " No hay ajos! — It has
no garlic! " they complained. Once or twice I acted
as agent between them and an under cook who
sneaked out of the galley with a roast chicken under
his jacket, but they grew visibly leaner day by day.

On the whole steerage life on the *New York* was
endurable. The third-class fare was on a par with
most English cooking,— well-meant but otherwise
uncommendable. The tables and dishes were moderately clean, the waiters, expecting a sixpence tip at
the end of the passage, were almost obliging. In
the steerage dining-room, large and airy, was a piano
around which we gathered of an evening to chat, or
to croak old-fashioned songs. Here it was that I
felt the full force of my long total abstinence from
English. It was days before I could talk fluently;
many a time my tongue clattered about a full half-
minute in quest of some quite everyday word.

On the fourth day out the oldest of the Spaniards
appealed to me for the twentieth time to intercede
for them with the third-class steward.

" Hombre," I answered, " it is useless; I have
talked myself hoarse. Go to him yourself and it
may have some effect."

" But he understands neither Castilian nor
Eúscarra! " cried the Basque.

" No matter," I replied. " He is a man in such
and such a uniform. When you run across him

touch him on the sleeve and lay your head sidewise on your hand — the pantomime for sleep the world over — and he will remember your case."

An hour or more afterward I was aroused from reading a book in an alleyway aft by the third-class steward.

" I say," he cried, " will you come and see what the bloomin' saints is biting these Spanish chaps? They ayn't no one else can chin their lingo."

I followed him forward.   Before the dispensary stood a wondering and sympathetic group, in the center of which was the Basque making wry faces and groaning, and the ship's surgeon looking almost frightened.

" What 's up? " I asked.

" Blow me if I know! " cried the medicine-man. " This chap comes and touches me on the arm and holds his hand against his cheek.   I gave him a dose for toothache, and the beggar 's been howling ever since.   Funny sort of creatures."

The Spaniards got no berth during the voyage, though I carried their appeal in person to the captain.   They were still encamped on the lower hatch on the morning when the land-fever drew us on deck at dawn.   Soon appeared a light-ship, then land, a view of the charred ruins of Coney Island, then a gasp of wonder from the emigrants as the sky-scrapers burst on their sight.   We steamed slowly up the harbor, checked by mail, custom, and doctor's boats, and tied up at a wharf early in the afternoon. Rain was pouring. I appeared before a commissioner in the second cabin to establish my nationality, bade the Basques farewell as they were leaving for Ellis Island, and scudded away through the deluge. In my pocket was exactly six cents. I caught up an evening paper and with the last coin in hand dived down into the Subway.

The Summer's Expense Account:

Transportation	$90.
Food and Lodging	55.
Bullfights, sights, souvenirs	10.
Miscellaneous	17.
	$172

$$\begin{array}{r} 2\,8'2 \\ 7\,8 \\ \hline 2\,1\,4 \end{array}$$